99 Blazing BBQ Recipes: Delicious Meals for Outdoor Cooking

Aroma Breeze Shis

Copyright © 2023 Aroma Breeze Shis
All rights reserved.

Contents

INTRODUCTION 7
1. Grilled Pineapple with Honey and Lime 8
2. Beer-Battered Onion Rings 8
3. Grilled Shrimp Skewers with Mango Salsa 9
4. Broiled Lobster Tail with Garlic Butter 10
5. Smoked Pork Ribs with BBQ Sauce 11
6. Grilled Zucchini Parmesan Fries 12
7. Grilled Chicken Breasts with Chimichurri Sauce 13
8. Grilled Veggie Quesadillas 14
9. Grilled Salmon with Lime-Cilantro Sauce 15
10. Grilled Halloumi Cheese with Mushrooms 15
11. Grilled Corn with Chipotle Butter 16
12. Grilled Eggplant with Roasted Garlic Spread 17
13. Grilled Flank Steak with Port Wine Glaze 18
14. Gralled S'mores with Chocalate Ganache 19
15. Grilled Stuffed Peppers with Rice and Cheese 20
16. Grilled Potato Nachos with Green Chili Sauce 21
17. Grilled Asparagus with Balsamic Glaze 22
18. Grilled Maple-Glazed Bacon Wraps 23
19. Grilled Fruit Kebabs with Honey-Lime Glaze 24
20. Grilled Street Tacos with Pickled Onions 25
21. Grilled Calamari with Lemon-Garlic Sauce 26
22. Grilled BBQ Pizza with Bacon and Chicken 27
23. Grilled Macaroni and Cheese Bites 27
24. Grilled Buffalo-Style Wings with Blue Cheese Dip 28
25. Grilled Pork Chops with Peach Salsa 29
26. Grilled Portobello Burgers with Spinach Pesto 30
27. Grilled Tuna with Mango Salsa 31

28. Grilled Pepper-Crusted Tuna Steaks 32
29. Grilled Vegetable Wraps with Hummus 33
30. Grilled Artichoke Hearts with Lemon Aioli 34
31. Grilled Lobster Tail with Coconut-Lime Butter 35
32. Grilled Shrimp Skewers with Tomato Basil Sauce 36
33. Grilled Quail with Kumquat Compote 37
34. Grilled Lamb Loin with Mint Chimichurri 38
35. Grilled Chorizo Sausage with Red Chimichurri 39
36. Grilled Fruit Skewers with Vanilla Yogurt 40
37. Grilled Chicken Caesar Wraps with Basil Pesto 41
38. Grilled Cornbread with Chipotle Butter 42
39. Grilled Tofu with Peanut Sauce 43
40. Grilled Chipotle-Lime Chicken Kabobs 44
41. Grilled Avocado Stuffed with Quinoa Salad 45
42. Grilled Eggplant Caprese Sandwiches 46
43. Grilled Salmon with Honey-Lime Glaze 48
44. Grilled Portobello Mushrooms with Balsamic Glaze 48
45. Grilled Cheese Sandwiches with Tomato Jam 49
46. Grilled Jerk Chicken Drumsticks 50
47. Grilled Cheese and Avocado Quesadillas 51
48. Grilled Halibut Fillets with Mango Salsa 52
49. Grilled Squash and Zucchini with Mango Sauce 53
50. Grilled Beer-Battered Fish and Chips 54
51. Grilled Lamb Kebabs with Mint Pesto 55
52. Grilled Polenta with Parmesan Cheese 56
53. Grilled Quinoa Stuffed Peppers 57
54. Grilled Potato Skins with Cheddar Cheese 58
55. Grilled Sweet Potato Hash with Chorizo 60
56. Grilled Apple and Brie Quesadillas 61

57. Grilled Asparagus and Mushroom Kebabs 61
58. Grilled Eggplant Burgers with Pesto 62
59. Grilled Pineapple with Chili-Lime Glaze 63
60. Grilled Orange-Ginger Pork Chops 64
61. Grilled Curried Vegetables with Peanuts 65
62. Grilled Vegetable Ratatouille with Goat Cheese 66
63. Grilled Coconut-Lime Chicken Breasts 67
64. Grilled Coconut-Lime Shrimp Skewers 68
65. Grilled Chicken Tostadas with Pickled Onions 69
66. Grilled Coconut-Ginger Salmon Steaks 70
67. Grilled Cornbread with Maple-Jalapeno Butter 71
68. Grilled Nectarine and Blue Cheese Salad 72
69. Grilled Feta and Tomato Kebabs 73
70. Grilled Eggplant and Roasted Red Pepper Sandwich 74
71. Grilled Flank Steak with Caramelized Onions 75
72. Grilled Balsamic-Glazed Portobello Mushroom 76
73. Grilled Whole Trout with Lemon-Ginger Butter 77
74. Grilled Bacon-Wrapped Beef Tenderloin 78
75. Grilled Mozzarella Sticks with Pesto 79
76. Grilled Potato Salad with Bacon and Sage 80
77. Grilled Chicken, Mushroom and Spinach Wraps 81
78. Grilled Peach Crumble with Cinnamon-Walnut Streusel 81
79. Grilled Gorgonzola and Sausage-Stuffed Mushrooms 83
80. Grilled Fish Tacos with Mango Salsa 84
81. Grilled Romaine and Avocado Salad 85
82. Grilled Watermelon Salad with Feta 85
83. Grilled Asparagus and Prosciutto Skewers 86
84. Grilled Chicken Caesar Salad Wraps 87
85. Grilled Cheese and Apple Kebabs 88

86. Grilled Artichoke and Tomato Bruschetta 89
87. Grilled Tilapia with Mango-Lime Salsa 90
88. Grilled Vegetable Skewers with Balsamic Glaze 91
89. Grilled Pineapple Bread Pudding with Rum-Caramel Sauce 92
90. Grilled Prosciutto-Wrapped Scallops 93
91. Grilled Corn on the Cob with Chili-Lime Butter 93
92. Grilled Potato Wedges with Garlic-Herb Butter 94
93. Grilled Kebabs with Apricot-Chipotle Glaze 95
94. Grilled Cheese Sandwich with Caramelized Onions 96
95. Grilled Tuna with Wasabi-Lime Mayonnaise 97
96. Grilled Spinach and Feta Salad 98
97. Grilled Fennel with Mascarpone Cheese 99
98. Grilled Pork Tenderloin with Orange-Honey Glaze 100
99. Grilled Banana Split with Chocolate Sauce 101
CONCLUSION 103

INTRODUCTION

Welcome to 99 Blazing Fire Pit Recipes: Delicious Meals for Outdoor Cooking! If you're looking for an exciting way to bring a new element to your outdoor cooking, you've come to the right place! Nothing brings people together like good food cooked over a blazing fire pit. This cookbook will provide you with step-by-step recipes for making delicious meals with your fire pit. As you cook, you'll enjoy the warmth and smokiness of the fire and the tantalizing aroma of the food being cooked around it.

Inside, you'll find a range of easy-to-follow recipes for a variety of meals that make use of your fire pit. These meal plans are designed to suit the different tastes of everyone in your family, no matter if you're cooking for two or for a large gathering. From breakfast dishes like breakfast tacos to dinner dishes like ribs, you'll find something to please everyone.

To get the most out of this cookbook, you'll need to be familiar with fire pit safety. For example, make sure you start with a strong, sturdy fire pit and use the proper fuel. You'll also want to make sure you're following all the rules of fire safety when it comes to extinguishing the fire and managing the flames. Additionally, make sure you're taking the proper precautions with food safety, like keeping raw and cooked foods separate and not cross-contaminating.

With this cookbook, you'll have a wealth of recipes and tips for cooking delicious meals over your open fire. Whether you're a novice griller or an experienced pit master, you're sure to find something to enjoy. So pick out your favorite recipe, rustle up the ingredients, and let's get cooking!

1. Grilled Pineapple with Honey and Lime

Grilled Pineapple with Honey and Lime is a sweet and zesty summer dish that delights your taste buds with its combination of flavors.

Serves 4, | Preparation Time 10 mins, | Ready in 10 mins.

Ingredients:
- 1/2 cup honey
- 3 tablespoons freshly squeezed lime juice
- 2 teaspoons vegetable oil
- 1/8 teaspoon salt
- 1/8 teaspoon freshly ground black pepper
- 2 large pineapple wedges, trimmed and sliced into 1/2inch thick rings

Instructions:
1. Preheat the grill to medium-high heat.
2. In a small bowl, whisk together the honey, lime juice, oil, salt, and pepper; set aside.
3. Grill the pineapple rings for 3 minutes on each side or until golden brown.
4. Brush each side of the pineapple with the honey lime glaze and continue grilling for 2 minutes on each side, or until the glaze is bubbly and caramelized.

Nutrition Information: Calories: 112 kcal, Carbohydrates: 28 g, Protein: 0.5 g, Fat: 1.7g, Saturated Fat: 0.3 g, Cholesterol: 0 mg, Sodium: 58 mg, Potassium: 89 mg, Fiber: 0.4g, Sugar: 25 g, Vitamin A: 80 IU, Vitamin C: 15.8 mg, Calcium: 8 mg, Iron: 0.2 mg.

2. Beer-Battered Onion Rings

Beer-Battered Onion Rings are a delicious and crunchy appetizer that make a great snack or side dish. This recipe yields 4 servings and takes approximately 25 minutes to prepare and 10 more minutes to cook.

Serving: 4| Preparation Time: 25 minutes| Ready Time: 10 minutes

Ingredients:
- 1 large onion
- 1 cup all-purpose flour
- 1 teaspoon of sea salt
- 1 teaspoon freshly ground pepper
- 12 ounces beer

Instructions:
1. Preheat oil in a deep-fryer to 375F.
2. Slice the onion into 1/4 inch thick rings and separate.
3. In a medium bowl, whisk together the flour, salt, pepper and beer.
4. Dip each onion ring into the batter and coat completely.
5. Carefully lower the onion rings into preheated oil and cook 3-4 at a time.
6. Fry until golden brown, about 2-3 minutes.
7. Transfer to a plate lined with paper towel to cool and absorb excess oil.

Nutrition Information:
Per serving: 290 calories; 5.2 g fat; 49.2 g carbohydrates; 4.4 g protein; 26 mg cholesterol; 494 mg sodium

3. Grilled Shrimp Skewers with Mango Salsa

Grilled Shrimp Skewers with Mango Salsa is a tropical-inspired dish that is perfect for summer barbecues. This summery and flavorful combo of shrimp, mango, and jalapeno makes it a perfect dish. Serve up some grilled shrimp skewers with a homemade mango salsa for your next barbecue!

Serving: 4| Preparation Time: 20 minutes| Ready Time: 25 minutes

Ingredients:
-1 lb of raw shrimp, shelled and deveined
-1 large mango, cubed
-1 jalapeno, seeded and minced
-2 tablespoons olive oil
-1 tablespoon lime juice

-Freshly chopped cilantro
-Salt to taste
-Skewers

Instructions:
1. Preheat the grill to medium-high heat.
2. In a bowl, mix together the cubed mango, jalapeno, olive oil, lime juice, and cilantro.
3. Thread the shrimp onto skewers, about 4-5 shrimp per skewer.
4. Place the shrimp skewers on the preheated grill, and cook for 4-5 minutes per side, until they are cooked through.
5. Serve the shrimp skewers with the mango salsa and enjoy!

Nutrition Information:
Calories: 269; Fat: 10.5g; Carbs: 21.5g; Protein: 21.6g; Sodium: 681.6mg

4. Broiled Lobster Tail with Garlic Butter

For an unforgettable seafood dinner, try this Broiled Lobster Tail with Garlic Butter. The slow cooked lobster tails are cooked in garlic butter and finished under the broiler for a delectable flavor and texture.

Serving: 4| Preparation Time: 5 minutes| Ready Time: 10 minutes

Ingredients:
-4 lobster tails
-4 tablespoons butter
-1 teaspoon minced garlic
-Salt and pepper to taste

Instructions:
1. Preheat the broiler.
2. Cut a slit in the topside of each lobster tail with kitchen scissors.
3. In a small saucepan, melt the butter with garlic over low heat.
4. Place the lobster tails on a sheet pan lined with foil and brush with the garlic butter.
5. Broil the lobster tails for 8 to 10 minutes until golden brown.
6. Season with salt and pepper, and serve.

Nutrition Information:
Calories: 324; Fat: 21 grams; Protein: 26 grams; Carbohydrates: 1 gram; Sodium: 272 milligrams.

5. Smoked Pork Ribs with BBQ Sauce

Smoked Pork Ribs with BBQ Sauce is a delicious and flavorful main dish that is perfect for summer barbecues. This dish requires minimal preparation and cooking time, yet gives a big reward in the form of juicy, smoky, and decadent pork ribs.

Serves 4. | Preparation Time: 10 minutes. | Ready in 1 hour and 25 minutes.

Ingredients:
- 5 lbs pork ribs
- 1 tablespoon smoked paprika
- 2 teaspoons garlic powder
- 2 teaspoons onion powder
- 1 teaspoon salt
- 1 teaspoon pepper
- 1/4 cup brown sugar
- 2 cups BBQ sauce

Instructions:
1. Preheat the oven to 400 degrees Fahrenheit.
2. Remove the membrane from the back of the ribs.
3. Mix together the smoked paprika, garlic powder, onion powder, salt, pepper and brown sugar in a bowl.
4. Rub the mixture all over the ribs and place on a baking sheet lined with foil.
5. Bake for 1 hour and 20 minutes.
6. Remove the ribs from the oven and brush with BBQ sauce and then return to the oven for an additional 5 minutes.
7. Remove the ribs from the oven and serve with extra BBQ sauce.

Nutrition Information:

Calories: 437
Fat: 23.2g
Carbohydrates: 12.8g
Protein: 43.5g

6. Grilled Zucchini Parmesan Fries

Grilled Zucchini Parmesan Fries are a tasty and healthy way to enjoy the flavour of Italian cuisine. These fries are light, crispy, and full of flavour.

Serving: Serves 4. | Preparation Time: 20 minutes. | Ready Time: 30 minutes.

Ingredients:
- 2 large zucchinis, sliced into thin strips
- 2 tablespoons olive oil
- 1/4 cup grated Parmesan cheese
- 2 tablespoons dried oregano
- 1 teaspoon salt
- Freshly ground black pepper

Instructions:
1. Preheat your grill to medium-high heat.
2. Place the zucchini strips in a large bowl. Drizzle with the olive oil and toss well.
3. In a small bowl, combine the Parmesan cheese, oregano, salt, and pepper.
4. Sprinkle the Parmesan mixture over the zucchini strips and toss to zoat.
5. Place the zucchini on the preheated grill and cook for about 10 minutes, flipping once.
6. Remove the zucchini from the grill and serve warm.

Nutrition Information: Per serving: 90 calories, 7g fat, 4g protein, 3g carbohydrates, 1g fiber, 200mg sodium.

7. Grilled Chicken Breasts with Chimichurri Sauce

This grilled chicken dish is a tasty, easy-to-make meal that doesn't take long to prepare. The marinated chicken breasts are bursting with flavor from the fresh chimichurri sauce, making for an unforgettable dinner.

Serving: 8 servings | Preparation Time: 15 minutes | Ready Time: 30 minutes

Ingredients:
- 8 chicken breasts
- 2 cloves of garlic, minced
- 2 tablespoons red wine vinegar
- 1 teaspoon sea salt
- 1 teaspoon freshly ground black pepper
- 1/2 cup olive oil
- 1/2 cup fresh parsley, finely chopped
- 1/3 cup fresh oregano, finely chopped
- 2 tablespoons fresh lemon juice
- 1/2 teaspoon red pepper flakes

Instruction:
1. Combine the garlic, red wine vinegar, sea salt, black pepper, olive oil, parsley, oregano, lemon juice, and red pepper flakes in a small bowl and stir until fully combined.
2. Place the chicken breasts in a shallow dish and pour the chimichurri marinade over them. Cover the dish and let the chicken marinate for at least 15 minutes.
3. Preheat a grill to medium-high heat.
4. Cook the chicken for 5-7 minutes on each side, or until cooked through.
5. Serve with remaining sauce on the side.

Nutrition Information:
Per serving: 345 calories; 23.0g fat; 2.6g saturated fat; 32.3g protein; 1.7g carbohydrates; 15.9mg cholesterol; 321mg sodium; 1.7g fiber.

8. Grilled Veggie Quesadillas

Grilled Veggie Quesadillas are delicious, savory, and packed with plant-based protein. These quesadillas are filled with mushrooms, bell peppers, onions, and black beans, and grilled to perfection.

Serving:Makes 4-6 quesadillas depending on the size | Preparation Time:20 minutes | Ready Time:15 minutes

Ingredients:
- 8 (6-inch) whole wheat tortillas
- 2 tablespoons olive oil
- 2 cups sliced mushrooms
- 2 bell peppers, (any color) diced
- 2 onions, diced
- 2 cups cooked black beans, drained and rinsed
- 2 cups Monterey Jack cheese, grated
- Chips and salsa, for serving

Instructions:
1. Heat a large skillet or grill pan over medium heat.
2. Brush each tortilla with some of the olive oil. Place the tortillas, oil side down, on the skillet.
3. Meanwhile, in a medium bowl, combine the mushrooms, bell peppers, onions, and black beans.
4. Once the first side of the tortillas are lightly browned, flip them over and place the veggie mixture on one half of each tortilla. Sprinkle the Monterey Jack cheese over the veggie mix.
5. Fold each tortilla in half and cook for 2-3 minutes on each side, or until the cheese is melted and the tortillas are golden brown.
6. Remove the quesadillas from the skillet and let cool slightly before serving. Serve with chips and salsa.

Nutrition Information:
Serving Size: 1 quesadilla
Calories: 179; Total Fat: 9g; Saturated Fat: 4g; Cholesterol: 19mg; Sodium: 349mg; Carbohydrates: 19g; Fiber: 4g; Sugar: 2g; Protein: 7g

9. Grilled Salmon with Lime-Cilantro Sauce

This Grilled Salmon with Lime-Cilantro Sauce is a delicious combination of flavors that the whole family will love! This easy dish is full of freshness and zest from the lime and cilantro, and the salmon is cooked to perfection on the grill.

Serving: 4-6 | Preparation Time: 15 minutes | Ready Time: 25 minutes

Ingredients:
- 2 lbs. salmon filet
- 1/3 cup olive oil
- 1/4 cup freshly squeezed lime juice
- 2 cloves garlic, minced
- 2 tablespoons freshly chopped cilantro
- 1 teaspoon salt
- 1/2 teaspoon black pepper

Instructions:
1. Preheat the grill to high heat.
2. Place the salmon filets on a greased grill and cook each side for 4-5 minutes, until the salmon is fully cooked.
3. Place the olive oil, lime juice, garlic, cilantro, salt, and pepper in a bowl and whisk until combined.
4. Remove the salmon from the grill and brush each side with the lime-cilantro sauce.
5. Serve the salmon with the remaining lime-cilantro sauce on top.

Nutrition Information (per serving):
Calories: 400, Fat: 23g, Carbs: 0g, Protein: 43g

10. Grilled Halloumi Cheese with Mushrooms

This Grilled Halloumi Cheese with Mushrooms dish is a fantastic vegan meal that is simple to make and full of flavor. The mushrooms are sautéed until golden brown and then combined with halloumi cheese and grilled to perfection.

Serving: Serves 4| Preparation Time: 10 minutes| Ready Time: 15 minutes

Ingredients:
- 250g halloumi cheese, sliced into 1 cm thick slices
- 300g mushrooms, sliced
- 1 tablespoon of olive oil
- Salt and pepper to taste

Instructions:
1. Heat a large skillet over medium-high heat.
2. Once the skillet is hot, add the olive oil and mushrooms.
3. Sauté the mushrooms until they have become golden brown and tender.
4. Reduce the heat to medium and add the halloumi slices.
5. Grill the halloumi until golden brown.
6. Serve the mushrooms and halloumi with salt and pepper, to taste.

Nutrition Information: Per Serving: Calories: 345, Total fat: 23g, Saturated fat: 10g, Cholesterol: 119mg, Sodium: 842mg, Total carbohydrate: 10g, Protein: 23g.

11. Grilled Corn with Chipotle Butter

This smoky Grilled Corn with Chipotle Butter is an easy way to add flavor and texture to corn on the cob. The recipe is made with just five simple ingredients and ready in under 30 minutes.

Serving: 4| Preparation Time: 5 minutes | Ready Time: 10 minutes

Ingredients:
- 4 ears of corn, husks and silks removed
- 2 tablespoons unsalted butter, melted
- 1–2 teaspoons of chipotle chili powder
- 1 tablespoon finely chopped cilantro
- Salt, to taste

Instructions:

1. Preheat grill to medium-high heat.
2. Spread the melted butter over the corn and sprinkle with the chipotle chili powder, cilantro and salt.
3. Grill the corn over medium-high heat for 8-10 minutes, turning the corn occasionally so that the sides get slightly charred.
4. Serve with extra chopped cilantro, if desired.

Nutrition Information (per serving):
Calories: 136; Fat: 8g; Carbs: 16g; Protein: 2g; Fiber: 2g; Sugar: 4g

12. Grilled Eggplant with Roasted Garlic Spread

This Grilled Eggplant with Roasted Garlic Spread is sure to be the hit of your next cookout. It's packed with flavor, and is sure to become an instant summer favorite.

Serving: 4-6 | Preparation Time: 25 minutes | Ready Time: 50 minutes

Ingredients:
- 2 large eggplant
- 2 potatoes, cubed
- 4 cloves garlic, peeled
- 1 teaspoon olive oil
- 1/4 teaspoon salt
- 1/4 teaspoon pepper
- 1/4 cup parsley, chopped
- 2 tablespoons mayonnaise
- 1 tablespoon lemon juice

Instructions:
1. Preheat grill to medium-high heat.
2. Cut the eggplant lengthwise into 1/2 inch slices.
3. Place eggplant slices, potatoes and garlic on a greased aluminum foil tray.
4. Drizzle olive oil over eggplant and potatoes and season with salt and pepper.

5. Place tray on preheated grill and cook for 25 minutes or until eggplant and potatoes are cooked through.
6. Meanwhile, in a small bowl, mix parsley, mayonnaise, and lemon juice to make a roasted garlic spread.
7. Once cooked, assemble eggplant slices by spreading a tablespoon of roasted garlic spread on each slice.
8. Serve.

Nutrition Information:
Calories: 273 kcal
Fat: 11.1 grams
Carbohydrates: 41.7 grams
Protein: 5.7 grams

13. Grilled Flank Steak with Port Wine Glaze

This delicious Grilled Flank Steak with Port Wine Glaze will make a great addition to any special occasion meal. The sweet and tangy glaze really complements the juicy steak, making it the perfect main entree.

Serving: 8 | Preparation Time: 10 minutes | Ready Time: 40 minutes

Ingredients:
- 2 pounds flank steak
- 2 cloves garlic, minced
- 2 tablespoons olive oil
- Salt and pepper to taste
- 2/3 cup port wine
- 2 tablespoons cold butter
- 2 tablespoons balsamic vinegar

Instructions:
1. Preheat grill to medium-high heat.
2. In a small bowl, mix together garlic, olive oil, salt, and pepper; rub mixture onto the steak.
3. Grill steak for 7 minutes on each side.
4. In a small saucepan, heat the port wine on medium heat. Simmer for 10 minutes, or until reduced by half.

5. Add butter and vinegar to the reduction. Stir until the butter has melted and the mixture is thick and syrupy.
6. Remove steak from grill and brush with the port wine glaze.
7. Allow steak to rest for 5 minutes before slicing.

Nutrition Information: Per serving: 286 calories, 16.7g fat, 5.1g saturated fat, 2.3g carbohydrates, 0.3g sugar, 27.1g protein

14. Gralled S'mores with Chocalate Ganache

Gooey, creamy and chocolatey, these Gralled S'mores with Chocolate Ganache are the epitome of indulgent treats! The dark chocolate pairs beautifully with the graham crackers, marshmallows and drizzle of ganache for a mouthwatering treat.

Serving: 6-8 | Preparation Time: 15 minutes | Ready Time: 25 minutes

Ingredients:
- 120g graham crackers
- 120g marshmallows
- 120g dark chocolate
- 150ml heavy cream
- 2 tablespoons sugar
- Vanilla extract

Instructions:
1. Preheat the oven to 220°C and place the graham crackers in a baking pan.
2. Put the marshmallows on top of the graham crackers and bake it in the oven for 15 minutes.
3. Once you take it out of the oven, let it cool down for 5 minutes.
4. Melt the dark chocolate in a double boiler.
5. Heat the heavy cream and sugar together in a small pot on medium heat until the sugar is dissolved.
6. Combine the mixture with melted chocolate and stir until combined.
7. Add a few drops of vanilla extract and set aside.
8. Place the graham crackers and marshmallows on a plate or board, and drizzle with the chocolate ganache.

Nutrition Information (per serving):
- Calories: 232 kcal
- Carbohydrates: 23g
- Protein: 2g
- Fat: 15g
- Sodium: 71mg

15. Grilled Stuffed Peppers with Rice and Cheese

Grilled Stuffed Peppers with Rice and Cheese are a delicious and healthy meal perfect for entertaining. This savory dish is packed with flavor, easy to make, and yields four servings. Prep time is 25 minutes and the ready time is 30 minutes.

Serving: 4 | Preparation Time: 25 minutes | Ready Time: 30 minutes

Ingredients:
- 4 bell peppers
- 1 cup cooked wild rice
- 1/2 cup diced zucchini
- 1 1/2 cup shredded mozzarella cheese
- 1 can (14.5 oz) diced tomatoes
- 1 teaspoon garlic powder
- Salt and pepper to taste

Instructions:
1. Preheat the grill to medium heat.
2. Slice the bell peppers in half and discard the stem and seeds. Place the peppers in a large bowl and set aside.
3. In a medium bowl, combine the cooked wild rice, diced zucchini, shredded cheese, diced tomatoes, garlic powder, salt, and pepper. Mix everything together until evenly combined.
4. Stuff each bell pepper half generously with the rice and cheese mixture. Place them on a large plate.
5. Place the stuffed peppers directly onto the preheated grill.
6. Grill the peppers for 25 minutes, flipping them once to ensure even cooking.

7. Remove the peppers from the grill, serve warm and enjoy!

Nutrition Information:
Calories: 310
Total Fat: 10g
Cholesterol: 20mg
Sodium: 510mg
Carbohydrates: 38g
Fiber: 5g
Protein: 16g

16. Grilled Potato Nachos with Green Chili Sauce

Grilled Potato Nachos with Green Chili Sauce is a flavorful and filling appetizer or snack, with a spicy-smoky-garlicky taste that packs a flavorful punch. The perfect dish for game nights, potlucks, and BBQs, this dish serves 4-6 and takes 30 minutes of | Preparation Time, with an additional 20-25 minutes for cooking time.

Serving: 4-6 | Preparation Time: 30 minutes | Ready Time: 20-25 minutes

Ingredients:
-1 lb of potatoes, sliced into rounds
-1 tablespoon of olive oil
-1/2 teaspoon of garlic powder
-2 teaspoons of smoked paprika
-1 teaspoon of chili powder
-Salt and pepper to taste
-1 cup of grated cheese
-1 (4-ounce) can of green chilies, drained
-1 tablespoon of freshly chopped cilantro
-2 tablespoons of olive oil
-1 cup of Favorite Nacho Cheese Sauce
-Lemon juice and sour cream, optional

Instructions:
1. Preheat the oven to 375F (190°C) and line a baking sheet with parchment paper.

2. Place the potato slices on the baking sheet, drizzle with olive oil, and season with garlic powder, smoked paprika, chili powder, salt, and pepper.
3. Bake for 20-25 minutes until potatoes are crispy and golden.
4. In a pan over medium-heat, heat olive oil and add green chilies, salt, and pepper. Stir for about 5 minutes until fragrant.
5. In a large bowl, combine the potatoes, grated cheese, green chili mixture, and cilantro.
6. Top the nachos with nacho cheese sauce and bake for an additional 5-10 minutes until cheese is melted and bubbly.
7. Serve the Grilled Potato Nachos with Green Chili Sauce with lemon juice, sour cream, and cilantro as a garnish.

Nutrition Information (per serving): Calories: 345, Total Fat: 18.5 g, Cholesterol: 28 mg, Sodium: 375 mg, Total Carbohydrates: 32.3 g, Protein: 11.5 g.

17. Grilled Asparagus with Balsamic Glaze

This Grilled Asparagus with Balsamic Glaze is an elegant, flavorful take on the classic vegetable side dish. For the perfect balance of sweetness and acidity, the asparagus is lightly seasoned with a balsamic reduction glaze that adds a delicious caramelized element. Ready to serve in 15 minutes, this dish provides a healthy and delicious meal for any day of the week.

Serving: 4 | Preparation Time: 5 minutes | Ready Time: 15 minutes

Ingredients:
- 1 lb asparagus
- 2 tsp olive oil
- 1 tsp sea salt
- 2 tbsp balsamic vinegar
- 2 tsp coconut sugar

Instructions:
1. Preheat the grill to medium-high heat.
2. Trim and wash the asparagus.

3. Place the asparagus on a large sheet of foil and drizzle with olive oil. Sprinkle with sea salt.
4. Gently fold the foil around the asparagus to create a packet.
5. Grill the asparagus for 8-10 minutes, flipping the packet halfway through the cooking time.
6. In a small saucepan over medium heat, whisk together the balsamic vinegar and coconut sugar until the sugar is dissolved and the mixture thickens.
7. Brush the asparagus generously with the glaze and serve.

Nutrition Information: Calories: 55; Protein: 2.4g; Carbohydrates: 5.9g; Total fat: 2.9g; Fiber: 2.8g; Sugar: 3.2g

18. Grilled Maple-Glazed Bacon Wraps

Grilled Maple-Glazed Bacon Wraps are a delicious combination of sweet and savory flavors, perfect for a summer BBQ or cookout. These wraps are surprisingly easy to make and only require a few ingredients.

Serves: 8 | Preparation Time: 10 minutes | Ready Time: 20 minutes

Ingredients:
- 16 strips of bacon
- 1/4 cup of maple syrup
- 1 teaspoon of black pepper
- 1 teaspoon of smoked paprika

Instructions:
1. Preheat the grill to medium heat.
2. In a small bowl, mix together the maple syrup, black pepper, and smoked paprika until fully combined.
3. Take 2 strips of bacon and wrap them around each other, using a toothpick to secure them together.
4. Brush the maple glaze over the bacon wrap.
5. Place the bacon wrap onto the preheated grill and cook for 10-15 minutes, flipping occasionally, until the bacon is fully cooked.
6. Remove the bacon wrap from the grill and enjoy.

Nutrition Information:
- Calories: 151
- Fat: 11.1g
- Carbohydrates: 7.8g
- Protein: 6.5g

19. Grilled Fruit Kebabs with Honey-Lime Glaze

Grilled Fruit Kebabs with Honey-Lime Glaze is a quick and delicious dessert with a subtle yet complimentary sweetness. It takes about ten minutes to prepare and fifteen minutes to cook, making it a perfect choice for any occasion. The glaze of honey and lime adds a sultry flavor to the skewered fruit.

Serving: 4| Preparation Time: 10 minutes| Ready Time: 15 minutes

Ingredients:
- 2 cups diced pineapple
- 2 cup cubed mango
- 2 cup cubed cantaloupe
- 2 tablespoons honey
- 1 tablespoon fresh lime juice

Instructions:
1. Preheat the grill over medium heat.
2. Thread the diced pineapple, mango and cantaloupe onto metal skewers.
3. Place the skewers on the hot grill and cook until slightly charred, about 5 minutes per side.
4. In a small bowl, mix together honey and lime juice.
5. Brush the cooked kebabs with the honey and lime glaze, turn and continue to grill for 2-3 minutes.

Nutrition Information: Per Serving (4 Servings): 120 calories, 0.5 g fat, 0 g saturated fat, 27 g carbohydrates, 1 g protein, 11 g sugars, 1 g fiber

20. Grilled Street Tacos with Pickled Onions

Grilled Street Tacos with Pickled Onions is a dish that takes the classic combination of tacos, grilled meats, and pickled vegetables to create a unique and satisfying meal. This delicious and easy-to-make recipe combines a savory chile-rubbed steak, grilled to perfection with sweet-and-sour pickled onions, housed and folded in a pair of warm and flavorful taco shells.

Serving: 4-6 | Preparation Time: 15 minutes | Ready Time: 45 minutes

Ingredients:
- 1 pound skirt steak
- 2 teaspoons ground Ancho chile or chili powder
- 2 teaspoons ground cumin
- 2 teaspoons kosher salt
- 1/4 teaspoon ground black pepper
- 2 tablespoons vegetable oil
- 1 cup white vinegar
- 1/2 cup honey
- 1/2 small red onion, thinly sliced
- 2 tablespoons minced garlic
- 12 (6-inch) corn tortillas
- 1/2 cup crumbled queso fresco, for serving

Instructions:
1. In a medium mixing bowl, combine the chile powder, cumin, salt, and pepper, and stir to combine. Rub the steak with the oil and the seasoning on all sides, then set aside.
2. In a medium saucepan, combine the vinegar, honey, onion, and garlic. Bring to a simmer over medium heat and cook for 15 minutes, or until the onions have softened.
3. Meanwhile, preheat a grill or grill pan to high heat. Grill the steak for 3 minutes on each side, or until the steak is cooked to your preferred doneness. Transfer the steak to a cutting board and let rest for 5 minutes before slicing against the grain into thin strips.
4. Heat the tortillas on the grill for 1-2 minutes per side until heated through.
5. To assemble the tacos, fill each tortilla with steak strips and top with pickled onions and crumbled queso fresco.

Nutrition Information:
Calories 250; Total fat 11 g; Saturated fat 3 g; Cholesterol 50 mg; Sodium 600 mg; Carbohydrate 16 g; Fiber 3 g; Protein 22 g.

21. Grilled Calamari with Lemon-Garlic Sauce

Grilled Calamari with Lemon-Garlic Sauce is a rich and delicious combination of flavors that will tantalize your taste buds. The slight char of the calamari pairs wonderfully with the acidic tang of the lemon juice, and the mellow garlic makes the perfect finishing touch.

Serves 4-6, | Preparation Time 10 minutes, | Ready time 15 minutes.

Ingredients:
- 1 lb calamari tubes, cleaned and sliced into thin rings
- 1 cup olive oil
- 4 cloves garlic, diced
- 2 lemons, juiced
- Salt and pepper to taste

Instructions:
1. Heat oil in a sauté pan over medium-high heat.
2. Gently add the calamari rings to the pan and reduce the heat to medium.
3. Cook the calamari for 3-4 minutes, stirring occasionally.
4. Add the garlic and cook for 1-2 minutes.
5. Add the lemon juice, salt, and pepper and mix together.
6. Cook for an additional 2-3 minutes.
7. Remove from heat and serve with lemon wedges.

Nutrition Information (per serving):
Calories: 301 kcal
Carbohydrates: 5.2 g
Fat: 25.9 g
Protein: 10.7 g
Sodium: 412 mg
Cholesterol: 155 mg

22. Grilled BBQ Pizza with Bacon and Chicken

Enjoy a delicious fusion of sweet and smoky flavors with this Grilled BBQ Pizza with Bacon and Chicken. This easy to make pizza is packed with flavor and sure to become a hit with your family.

Serving: 4 servings | Preparation Time: 10 minutes | Ready Time: 20 minutes

Ingredients:
-1 pre-baked pizza crust
-1/2 cup BBQ sauce
-1 1/2 cups cooked shredded chicken
-3/4 cup cooked and crumbled bacon
-1 cup shredded mozzarella cheese
-1/3 cup diced red onion

Instructions:
1. Preheat your grill for medium heat.
2. Spread BBQ sauce over the pre-baked pizza crust.
3. Top with chicken, bacon, cheese and onion.
4. Place pizza on the grill, cover and cook for 8-10 minutes. Make sure to watch the pizza and turn it over a couple of times during cooking.
5. Remove from the grill and cut into slices.

Nutrition Information: Calories: 722; Fat: 29 g; Carbohydrates: 71 g; Protein: 42 g; Cholesterol: 83 mg; Sodium: 1405 mg.

23. Grilled Macaroni and Cheese Bites

Delicious and easy to make, these Grilled Macaroni and Cheese Bites are a great summer treat! Combining mild, creamy cheese and bite-sized macaroni pasta, these bites are a perfect snack for picnics, potlucks, or BBQs.

Serving: Makes 24 bites | Preparation Time: 15 minutes | Ready Time: 15 minutes

Ingredients:
- 8oz elbow macaroni pasta
- 1/2 cup shredded cheddar cheese
- 1/2 cup shredded Monterey Jack cheese
- 4 tablespoons butter
- 2 tablespoons heavy cream
- Salt

Instructions:
1. Bring a large pot of water to a boil and cook the elbow macaroni for about 6 minutes, or according to package directions.
2. Drain the noodles and transfer them to a large bowl. Stir in the butter, cheddar cheese, Monterey Jack cheese, and heavy cream until everything is well combined. Add salt to taste.
3. Take a spoonful of the macaroni and cheese mixture and shape it into a small ball. Repeat until you've used up all the mixture.
4. Preheat the grill to medium-high heat.
5. Place the ball on a greased grill grates. Grill for 4-5 minutes, flipping occasionally until the balls are lightly charred and crispy.

Nutrition Information: Per serving: 140 calories, 8g fat, 0.4g saturated fat, 2g sugar, 7g protein.

24. Grilled Buffalo-Style Wings with Blue Cheese Dip

Enjoy the wonderful blend of spice and tang with these delicious Grilled Buffalo-Style Wings with Blue Cheese Dip. This perfect dish for game day will leave your guests wanting more.

Serving: 6 | Preparation Time: 10 minutes | Ready Time: 40 minutes

Ingredients:
- 18 chicken wings
- 2 tablespoons cooking oil

- 3 tablespoons butter
- 2 tablespoons Worcestershire sauce
- 2 teaspoons garlic powder
- 2 teaspoons onion powder
- 2 tablespoons cayenne pepper
- 1 cup hot sauce
- 2 tablespoons white vinegar
- 1/4 cup blue cheese crumbles
- 2 tablespoons chives, chopped

Instructions:
1. Preheat the oven to 450° F.
2. Place the wings on a baking tray and drizzle with the cooking oil.
3. Bake for 20 minutes, flipping the wings once halfway.
4. In a small saucepan, melt the butter and stir in the Worcestershire sauce, garlic powder, onion powder, cayenne pepper, hot sauce and white vinegar.
5. Remove the wings from the oven and coat with the sauce.
6. Place the wings onto a hot grill on medium-high heat and grill for 15 minutes, flipping frequently.
7. In a small bowl, combine the blue cheese crumbles and chives.
8. Serve the wings warm with the blue cheese dip.

Nutrition Information:
Calories: 655; Total Fat: 51g; Saturated Fat: 19g; Cholesterol: 173mg; Sodium: 2055mg; Total Carbohydrates: 11g; Dietary Fiber: 1g; Protein: 40g

25. Grilled Pork Chops with Peach Salsa

Grilled Pork Chops with Peach Salsa is an easy to make, delicious grilled dish that is perfect for a summertime cookout! With this flavor combination of pork and peaches, you'll be sure to please any crowd.

Serving: 4| Preparation Time: 15 minutes| Ready Time: 30 minutes

Ingredients:
- 4 boneless pork chops

- 2 tablespoons olive oil
- 2 teaspoons garlic powder
- 2 teaspoons paprika
- 2 peaches, diced
- 1/4 red onion, diced
- 2 tablespoons chopped cilantro
- 2 tablespoons lime juice
- 1 tablespoon honey
- Salt and pepper to taste

Instructions:
1. Preheat your grill to medium-high heat.
2. Rub the pork chops with olive oil, garlic powder, and paprika.
3. Place the pork chops on the grill for 4-5 minutes per side, or until cooked through.
4. In a medium-sized bowl, combine the diced peaches, red onion, cilantro, lime juice, honey, and a pinch of salt and pepper; stir until combined.
5. Serve the pork chops with a generous scoop of the peach salsa.

Nutrition Information:
Calories: 294; Total Fat: 12.4g; Carbohydrates: 10.4g; Protein: 33.8g; Sodium: 821mg; Fiber: 1.2g

26. Grilled Portobello Burgers with Spinach Pesto

This delicious and hearty Grilled Portobello Burgers with Spinach Pesto make for a great vegetarian option for barbeques, potlucks, or weeknight dinners. This pesto-infused recipe is sure to be a crowd-pleaser and a great way to get more antioxidants, vitamins, and minerals into your diet.

Serving: 4| Preparation Time: 15 minutes| Ready Time: 25 minutes

Ingredients:
- 4 large portobello mushrooms, stems removed
- 2 tablespoons of olive oil
- Salt and pepper to taste
- 1 cup chopped fresh baby spinach leaves

- 2 cloves of garlic, minced
- 2 tablespoons of fresh basil leaves
- 2 tablespoons of fresh parsley leaves
- 2 tablespoons of toasted pine nuts
- 2 tablespoons of olive oil
- 2 tablespoons of freshly grated Parmesan cheese
- 4 hamburger buns (optional)

Instructions:
1. Preheat the grill to medium-high heat.
2. Brush the mushroom caps on both sides with the 2 tablespoons of olive oil. Sprinkle with salt and pepper.
3. Place the mushrooms on the grill and cook for about 5 minutes per side, or until tender.
4. In a food processor or blender, add the spinach, garlic, basil, parsley, pine nuts, 2 tablespoons of olive oil, Parmesan cheese, and a little salt and pepper. Blend together until evenly incorporated.
5. Toast the buns, if desired.
6. Assemble the burgers and top each patty with some of the spinach pesto.
7. Serve the burgers on the toasted buns and enjoy.

Nutrition Information:
Calories: 156; Total Fat: 9.4 g; Cholesterol: 2.6 mg; Sodium: 216 mg; Total Carbohydrates: 12 g; Dietary Fiber: 4.1 g; Protein: 5.8 g.

27. Grilled Tuna with Mango Salsa

This easy-to-make Grilled Tuna with Mango Salsa is a delicious and healthy way to switch up your weekly dinner menu. Served over your favorite greens, it's perfect for a summertime meal.

Serving: 4 | Preparation Time: 10 minutes | Ready Time: 15 minutes

Ingredients:
- 2 tuna steaks
- 1 tbsp olive oil
- 1 teaspoon paprika

- 1/2 teaspoon garlic powder
- 3 limes
- Mango Salsa
- 2 ripe mangos, diced
- 1/4 red onion, diced
- 1/4 cup cilantro leaves, roughly chopped
- 2 limes, juiced
- Salt and pepper to taste

Instructions:
1. Preheat your grill to medium-high heat.
2. Rub the tuna steaks with the olive oil, paprika, and garlic powder. Grill for about 2 minutes on each side or until steaks reach your desired temperature.
3. Squeeze the juice from 2 of the limes onto the tuna steaks and let them rest.
4. Place the diced mango, red onion, cilantro, and juice from the remaining 1 lime in a bowl and mix together until combined. Season with salt and pepper to taste.
5. Serve the tuna steaks over greens and top with the mango salsa. Enjoy!

Nutrition Information:
Calories: 248; Total Fat: 7grams; Carbohydrates: 29grams; Protein: 16grams; Cholesterol: 33milligrams; Sodium: 144milligrams.

28. Grilled Pepper-Crusted Tuna Steaks

This Grilled Pepper-Crusted Tuna Steaks dish is a perfect combination of seared tuna with a crunchy pepper crust, making a delicious and unique meal.

Serves 4, | Preparation Time 10 minutes, | Ready time 15 minutes.

Ingredients:
- 4 tuna steaks
- 1/2 cup of crushed black pepper
- 2 tablespoons of olive oil
- Salt to taste

Instructions:
1. Preheat your grill to high heat and brush lightly with oil to prevent sticking.
2. In a shallow dish, combine the pepper, olive oil and salt and stir to combine.
3. Dip each tuna steak into the pepper mixture and place onto the hot grill.
4. Sear for about 5 minutes, flipping once until the tuna steak is evenly crusted.
5. Serve with a side salad of your choice.

Nutrition Information: Per Serving – Calories: 187, Total Fat: 6.6g, Cholesterol: 83mg, Sodium: 142mg, Total Carbs: 2.6g, Protein: 25.2g

29. Grilled Vegetable Wraps with Hummus

Grilled Vegetable Wraps with Hummus: These savory and delicious wraps are a perfect, quick and easy meal for any day of the week. With crunchy grilled vegetables and creamy hummus, you are sure to enjoy every bite!

Serving: 4| Preparation Time: 15 minutes| Ready Time: 15 minutes

Ingredients:
- 4 large flour tortillas
- 1 red bell pepper, sliced
- 1 yellow bell pepper, sliced
- 1 small zucchini, sliced
- 1 small red onion, thinly sliced
- 1/2 teaspoon garlic powder
- Olive oil
- 2 tablespoons balsamic vinegar
- 1 cup hummus
- 2 tablespoons finely chopped parsley, plus extra for garnish

Instructions:

1. Preheat a grill or large grill pan to medium-high heat.
2. Place bell peppers, zucchini, and red onion in a large bowl. Drizzle with olive oil and balsamic vinegar, sprinkle with garlic powder and toss to coat vegetables evenly. Grill vegetables until lightly charred and tender, about 5-7 minutes.
3. Heat the tortillas in a large dry skillet over medium heat until warm and lightly golden, about 1 minute per side.
4. Spread each tortilla with one-fourth cup hummus. Top with grilled vegetables and sprinkle with parsley. Roll each wrap up and place in a serving dish. Garnish with more parsley and serve.

Nutrition Information:
Calories: 297; Total fat: 11g; Saturated fat: 1g; Polyunsaturated fat: 3.5g; Monounsaturated fat: 5.5g; Cholesterol: 0mg; Sodium: 287mg; Potassium: 372mg; Carbohydrate: 36g; Dietary fiber: 6.3g; Sugar: 5.6g; Protein: 9.3g.

30. Grilled Artichoke Hearts with Lemon Aioli

Grilled Artichoke Hearts with Lemon Aioli is an easy, delicious and healthy way to enjoy the flavors of artichokes. This recipe is vegan, gluten-free and paleo-friendly, and perfect for a summer barbecue.

Serving: 4 | Preparation Time: 10 minutes | Ready Time: 20 minutes

Ingredients:
- 2 tablespoons olive oil
- 2 cloves garlic, crushed
- 2 tablespoons fresh lemon juice
- 1/4 cup vegan mayonnaise
- 2 cans artichoke hearts, drained and halved
- Salt and pepper

Instructions:
1. Preheat the grill to medium-high heat.
2. In a small bowl, whisk together the olive oil, garlic, lemon juice and vegan mayo to make the aioli.

3. Place the artichoke hearts on the grill and cook for 10 minutes, flipping once halfway through.
4. Remove from the grill, season with salt and pepper, and drizzle with the lemon aioli.

Nutrition Information:
Serving size: 4
Calories: 150
Total Fat: 9.9 g
Saturated Fat: 0.9 g
Cholesterol: 0 mg
Sodium: 349.1 mg
Carbohydrates: 11.8 g
Fiber: 5.7 g
Sugar: 0 g
Protein: 3.2 g

31. Grilled Lobster Tail with Coconut-Lime Butter

This delicious Grilled Lobster Tail with Coconut-Lime Butter is a surefire crowd-pleaser. With its flavorful combination of sweet shrimp and coconut-lime butter, it is sure to be the highlight of the meal.

Serving: Servings: 4 | Preparation Time: Preparation Time: 10 minutes | Ready Time:Ready Time: 20 minutes

Ingredients:
- 4 (7-ounce) lobster tails
- 4 tablespoons butter, melted
- 2 tablespoons unsweetened coconut flakes
- 1 tablespoon lime zest
- 2 teaspoons lime juice
- Salt, to taste

Instructions:
1. Preheat the grill to medium-high heat.

2. Split each lobster tail in half, lengthwise, and press the meat up so it is exposed.
3. In a medium bowl, mix together the melted butter, coconut flakes, lime zest, and lime juice.
4. Brush the butter mixture on top of the lobster tails, and season with salt.
5. Place the lobster tails, butter-side-up, on the grill and cook for 8 to 10 minutes.
6. Serve the lobster tails while they are still hot and enjoy!

Nutrition Information:
Per serving: 241 calories; 18.1g fat; 1.9g carbohydrates; 20.2g protein.

32. Grilled Shrimp Skewers with Tomato Basil Sauce

Grilled Shrimp Skewers with Tomato Basil Sauce is a zesty and colorful dish that's perfect for any summer BBQ or outdoor gathering. The sweet and savory tomato basil sauce will have everyone coming back for seconds!

Serving: 4| Preparation Time: 10 minutes| Ready Time: 20 minutes

Ingredients:
– 1 lb large shrimp, peeled, deveined, and tails-on
– 1/4 cup olive oil
– 1 teaspoon garlic powder
– 2 tablespoons balsamic vinegar
– 2 tablespoons chopped fresh basil
– 2 tablespoons chopped fresh oregano
– 2 tablespoons tomato paste
– Salt and pepper to taste
– 8 skewers

Instructions:
1. Begin by prepping the shrimp by removing the shells and tails.
2. In a bowl, mix the olive oil, garlic powder, balsamic vinegar, basil, oregano, tomato paste, salt, and pepper.

3. Place the shrimp in the bowl and mix with the marinade. Let it sit for 10 minutes.
4. Heat your grill to medium-high heat and soak the skewers in water for 5 minutes.
5. Place the shrimp on the skewers and grill for about 4 minutes per side.
6. Serve with warm tomato basil sauce.

Nutrition Information:
Serving size: 1 skewer
Calories: 145
Total Fat: 7 g
Saturated Fat: 1 g
Cholesterol: 121 mg
Sodium: 203 mg
Total Carbohydrate: 7 g
Protein: 10 g

33. Grilled Quail with Kumquat Compote

Grilled Quail with Kumquat Compote is a delicious and flavorful dish that combines earthy flavors of grilled quail with the bright, tart-sweet flavors of kumquat compote. It's a simple yet impressive main course that is sure to create an unforgettable culinary experience.

Serving: 4| Preparation Time: 15 minutes| Ready Time: 25 minutes

Ingredients:
- 4 quail, thawed and patted dry
- 2 tablespoons of olive oil
- Salt & pepper to taste
- 2 cups of kumquats, pitted and quartered
- 1/2 cup of sugar
- 1/2 cup of white wine
- 1/4 cup of fish sauce

Instructions:
1. Preheat the grill to medium-high heat.
2. Rub the quail with olive oil and season with salt and pepper.

3. Grill the quail for 6 to 8 minutes, turning once or twice.
4. In a medium saucepan, combine the kumquats, sugar, wine, and fish sauce.
5. Bring the mixture to a simmer over medium heat and stir occasionally until the kumquats soften and the mixture thickens up slightly.
6. Serve the quail topped with the kumquat compote.

Nutrition Information (per serving):
Calories: 501, Protein: 33 g, Fat: 24 g, Carbohydrates: 27 g, Sodium: 924 mg, Sugar: 21 g.

34. Grilled Lamb Loin with Mint Chimichurri

This Grilled Lamb Loin with Mint Chimichurri is a hearty and flavorful entrée that will satisfy even the pickiest of eaters! It only takes an hour to prepare and the recipe yields 4 servings. An added bonus, it's packed with a significant amount of protein and healthy fat.

Serving: 4 | Preparation Time: 10 minutes| Ready Time: 50 minutes

Ingredients:
• Lamb loin – 8 pieces
• Olive oil – 1/4 cup
• Sea salt – 2 teaspoons
• Ground black pepper – 2 teaspoons
• Oregano – 1 teaspoon
• Mint leaves – 1/2 cup, chopped
• Garlic – 3 cloves, minced
• Red onions – 2 tablespoons, chopped
• Red wine vinegar – 1 tablespoon
• Parsley – 1/4 cup, chopped
• Sun-dried tomatoes – 1/4 cup

Instructions:
1. Preheat your outdoor grill over medium-high heat.
2. Meanwhile, coat the lamb loin with olive oil, salt, pepper, and oregano in a bowl.

3. Place the lamb onto the pre-heated grill and cook for about 10 minutes, flipping halfway through.
4. In another bowl, combine the mint leaves, garlic, red onions, red wine vinegar, parsley, and sun-dried tomatoes.
5. Once the lamb is cooked, top each piece with a spoonful of the mint chimichurri and serve.

Nutrition Information (Per Serving):
Calories – 240, Total Fat – 8g, Saturated Fat – 3g, Cholesterol – 105mg, Sodium – 210mg, Total Carbohydrate – 5g, Dietary Fiber – 1g, Protein – 28g

35. Grilled Chorizo Sausage with Red Chimichurri

This Grilled Chorizo Sausage with Red Chimichurri is perfect for any tasty get-together! Carefully spiced with chili, garlic, and other aromatic herbs, the slightly smoky flavor of chorizo pairs perfectly with a zesty, fresh chimichurri sauce. This mouthwatering dish is the ideal accompaniment to any outdoor barbecue.

Serving: 4 | Preparation Time: 10 minutes | Ready Time: 25 minutes

Ingredients:
-4 chorizo sausages
-2 tablespoons extra-virgin olive oil
-4 cloves garlic, minced
-2 tablespoons chili powder
-2 teaspoons smoked paprika
-2 tablespoons red wine vinegar
-1 cup chopped parsley
-1/4 cup extra-virgin olive oil
-1/4 cup dried oregano
-2 tablespoons freshly squeezed lemon juice

Instructions:
1. Preheat the grill to medium-high heat.
2. Place the chorizo sausages on the grill, and cook, turning occasionally, until fully cooked, about 12 minutes.

3. Meanwhile, heat 2 tablespoons of olive oil in a small skillet over medium heat.
4. Add the garlic, chili powder, and smoked paprika, and cook, stirring, until fragrant, 1-2 minutes.
5. Add the red wine vinegar, and bring to a simmer.
6. Remove the skillet from the heat and set aside.
7. In a medium bowl, combine the parsley, 1/4 cup of olive oil, oregano, lemon juice, and the chili garlic mixture and mix.
8. Transfer the grilled sausages onto a plate and top them with the red chimichurri sauce.

Nutrition Information:
Calories: 272; Total Fat: 23 g; Saturated Fat: 5 g; Protein: 9 g; Carbohydrate: 6 g; Fiber: 1 g; Sugars: 1 g; Sodium: 310 mg.

36. Grilled Fruit Skewers with Vanilla Yogurt

The perfect dessert for a hot, summer day, Grilled Fruit Skewers with Vanilla Yogurt is sure to be a hit with the whole family. The combination of sweet, juicy, grilled fruit and creamy vanilla yogurt is sure to tantalize taste buds and delight guests. Serve this easy dish as a dessert, and with some nutritious fruits on the skewer, you can feel good about feeding it to your family and friends!

Serving: 4-6 | Preparation Time: 10 minutes | Ready Time: 20 minutes

Ingredients:
-1 pint strawberries, hulled and cut into halves
-1 pineapple, cut into cubes
-1 mango, cut into cubes
-2 oranges, cut into wedges
-Wooden or metal skewers
-1 cup plain yogurt
-1 teaspoon vanilla extract
-2 tablespoons honey

Instructions:
1. Preheat a grill to medium-high heat.

2. Thread the fruit onto the skewers, alternating between different types as desired.
3. Grill the skewers for 4-6 minutes, rotating occasionally to get an even char on all sides.
4. Meanwhile, in a small bowl, mix together the yogurt, vanilla extract, and honey until well combined.
5. Serve the grilled fruit skewers with the vanilla yogurt for dipping.

Nutrition Information:
Calories: 146
Carbohydrates: 34g
Protein: 4g
Fat: 1g
Saturated Fat: 0g
Cholesterol: 3mg
Sodium: 20mg
Potassium: 370mg
Fiber: 5g
Sugar: 28g

37. Grilled Chicken Caesar Wraps with Basil Pesto

These Grilled Chicken Caesar Wraps with Basil Pesto are the perfect combination of flavor-packed ingredients to create a delicious meal! Enjoy the crunch of the lettuce, the zesty Caesar dressing, and the homemade basil pesto paired with the flavor of crispy, grilled chicken.

Serving Size: 4| Preparation Time: 10 minutes | Ready Time: 20 minutes

Ingredients:
- 4 large wrap or flatbreads
- 600g chicken breast, cooked and thinly sliced
- 2 tsp olive oil
- head romaine lettuce, cut into strips
- 2 avocados, cubed
- 1/3 cup Caesar salad dressing
- 1 cup basil pesto
- 1/4 cup shaved parmesan cheese

Instructions:
1. Preheat a grill or frying pan over medium-high heat.
2. Brush the chicken slices lightly with oil and place on the preheated pan or grill. Cook for about 8 minutes, flipping once, until lightly golden and cooked through. Set aside.
3. Place the wraps or flatbreads on a flat surface. Layer each with lettuce strips, avocado cubes, Caesar salad dressing, two chicken slices, a tablespoon of basil pesto, and sprinkle some parmesan.
4. Finally, fold each wrap into a burrito-style wrap and enjoy.

Nutrition Information (per wrap):
Calories: 400
Total fat: 18g
Saturated fat: 5g
Cholesterol: 79mg
Sodium: 840mg
Carbohydrate: 27g
Fiber: 5g
Sugar: 4g
Protein: 32g

38. Grilled Cornbread with Chipotle Butter

Grilled Cornbread with Chipotle Butter is a flavorful, smoky and sweet twist on traditional cornbread. It's a satisfying side dish that's packed with delicious flavor.

Servings: 8 | Preparation Time: 10 minutes | Ready Time: 25 minutes

Ingredients:
- 1 cup yellow cornmeal
- 1 cup all-purpose flour
- 1 tablespoon sugar
- 1 teaspoon baking powder
- 1 teaspoon baking soda
- 1/2 teaspoon salt
- 1 cup buttermilk

- 4 tablespoons melted butter
- 2 eggs
- 10-15 chipotle peppers in adobo sauce, finely chopped
- 2 tablespoons butter, melted

Instructions:
1. Preheat the grill to medium-high heat.
2. In a large bowl, mix together the cornmeal, flour, sugar, baking powder, baking soda, and salt.
3. In a separate bowl, whisk together the buttermilk, melted butter, and eggs.
4. Pour the wet ingredients into the dry ingredients and mix until just combined.
5. In a small bowl, mix together the finely chopped chipotle peppers and melted butter.
6. Grease an 8-inch cast iron skillet and pour half of the batter into the skillet.
7. Spoon the chipotle butter mixture over the batter in the skillet.
8. Top with the remaining batter.
9. Place the skillet on the preheated grill and cover with a lid or aluminum foil.
10. Cook for 15-20 minutes, or until the edges of the cornbread are golden brown.
11. Remove from the heat and allow to cool for 5 minutes before serving.

Nutrition Information (per serving):
Calories: 206, Total Fat: 8 g, Saturated Fat: 5 g, Cholesterol: 42 mg, Sodium: 335 mg, Carbohydrates: 27 g, Dietary Fiber: 1 g, Sugars: 3 g, Protein: 4 g.

39. Grilled Tofu with Peanut Sauce

Grilled Tofu with Peanut Sauce is a simple vegan recipe that is packed with flavor and perfect for a light dinner. This meal serves two people, takes fifteen minutes to prepare, and will be ready to serve in fifteen minutes.

Serving: 2 | Preparation Time: 15 minutes | Ready Time: 15 minutes

Ingredients:
- 200g firm tofu, cubed
- 2 garlic cloves, finely chopped
- 2 tablespoons vegetable oil
- 3 tablespoons creamy peanut butter
- 2 tablespoons soy sauce
- 1 tablespoon brown sugar
- 2 tablespoons lime juice
- 2 tablespoons chopped unsalted peanuts

Instructions:
1. Preheat the oven to 375F.
2. Place the cubed tofu on a parchment-lined baking sheet and bake for 10 minutes then set aside.
3. In a small saucepan, heat olive oil over medium-high heat. Add garlic and sauté until fragrant, about 1-2 minutes.
4. Add peanut butter, soy sauce, brown sugar, and lime juice. Cook and stir until ingredients are combined and heated through.
5. Add in the cooked tofu to the peanut sauce and stir to combine.
6. Heat for an additional 2-3 minutes and top with peanuts.
7. Serve hot over steamed or roasted vegetables.

Nutrition Information (per serving): Total Calories: 477, Total Fat: 34g, Saturated Fat: 6g, Total Carbohydrates: 18g, Protein: 24g, Fiber: 4g, Sodium: 844mg.

40. Grilled Chipotle-Lime Chicken Kabobs

Enjoy a delicious and spicy fiesta with these Grilled Chipotle-Lime Chicken Kabobs. The perfect combination of grilled chicken, juicy bell peppers, sweet pineapple, and zesty lime marinade is sure to tantalize the taste buds. This dish is an ideal summer barbeque entrée that is both quick and easy.

Serving: 8 | Preparation Time: 20 minutes | Ready Time: 30 minutes

Ingredients:
- 2 chicken breasts, cubed
- 1 red bell pepper, cubed
- 1 yellow bell pepper, cubed
- 1 green bell pepper, cubed
- 1 pineapple, cubed
- 1 lime
- 3 cloves garlic, minced
- 3 tablespoons olive oil
- 1 teaspoon chipotle powder
- 1 teaspoon chili powder
- 1 teaspoon onion powder
- Salt and pepper to taste

Instructions:
1. In a large bowl, combine the cubed chicken breasts, bell peppers, and pineapple.
2. In a separate bowl, whisk together the lime juice, garlic, olive oil, chipotle powder, chili powder, onion powder, salt and pepper.
3. Pour the marinade over the chicken and vegetable mixture. Toss to coat. Cover and let marinate in the refrigerator for 20 minutes.
4. Preheat the grill to medium-high heat.
5. Assemble 8 skewers with the marinated chicken, bell peppers, and pineapple.
6. Grill the kabobs for 8-10 minutes, flipping once, until chicken is cooked through and vegetables are tender.

Nutrition Information (per serving): Calories: 178 Fat: 7g Carbohydrates: 11g Protein: 17g

41. Grilled Avocado Stuffed with Quinoa Salad

This Grilled Avocado Stuffed with Quinoa Salad is a healthy and delicious meal that is easy to whip up and perfect for any occasion! It is packed with nutritious and flavorful ingredients like quinoa, feta cheese, cherry tomatoes, and herbs. The avocado shell is grilled and stuffed with a salad of quinoa, making it a hearty and flavorful protein-packed dish.

Serving: 4-6 | Preparation Time: 15 minutes | Ready Time: 25 minutes

Ingredients:
- 2 large avocados
- 2 cups cooked quinoa
- 1/3 cup crumbled feta cheese
- 1/2 cup cherry tomatoes, cut in half
- 2 tablespoons olive oil
- 2 tablespoons fresh herbs (such as parsley, mint, or basil)
- Salt and pepper, to taste

Instruction:
1. Preheat a grill pan over medium-high heat. Slice avocados in half and scoop out some of the flesh from the center of each half.
2. In a medium bowl, combine quinoa, feta cheese, cherry tomatoes, olive oil, herbs, salt, and pepper. Mix well.
3. Stuff the grilled avocado halves with the quinoa mixture.
4. Place the stuffed avocados on the preheated grill. Grill for 3-5 minutes, flipping over once.
5. Serve hot.

Nutrition Information: (per serving)
Calories: 294 kcal
Fat: 16.8 g
Carbohydrates: 29.2 g
Protein: 7.7 g

42. Grilled Eggplant Caprese Sandwiches

Grilled Eggplant Caprese Sandwiches is a delicious twist on Caprese salad, combining grilled eggplant, tart balsamic reduction, mozzarella cheese, and fragrant basil to create a flavorful and satisfying vegetarian sandwich.

Serving: 4 to 6 sandwiches | Preparation Time: 10 minutes | Ready Time: 30 minutes

Ingredients:
- 3 tablespoons olive oil
- 2 large eggplants (about 2 1/2 lbs), cut into 1/2-inch thick slices
- 4-6 ciabatta rolls, split
- 1/2 cup balsamic vinegar
- 2 tablespoons honey
- 6 ounces fresh mozzarella cheese, sliced
- 1 cup fresh basil leaves
- Salt and freshly ground pepper

Instructions:
1. Heat 1 tablespoon of the olive oil in a large grill pan over medium-high heat.
2. Working in batches, add the eggplant slices and cook, turning occasionally, until charred on both sides, about 10 minutes.
3. Meanwhile, in a small saucepan, bring the balsamic vinegar and honey to a boil, reduce the heat and simmer until slightly thickened, about 8 minutes.
4. Brush the bottom halves of the rolls with the remaining 2 tablespoons of olive oil.
5. Arrange the grilled eggplant, mozzarella, and basil leaves on top of the bread.
6. Drizzle with the balsamic reduction, season with salt and pepper, then top with the remaining roll.
7. Grill the sandwiches in the same grill pan over medium-high heat until lightly browned and the cheese is melted, about 3 minutes per side. Serve warm.

Nutrition Information (per sandwich):
- 284 calories
- 13 g fat
- 5 g saturated fat
- 327 mg sodium
- 30 g carbohydrates
- 5 g fiber
- 13 g sugar
- 10 g protein

43. Grilled Salmon with Honey-Lime Glaze

Enjoy the delicious combination of sweet honey and tangy lime in this flavorful and easy Grilled Salmon with Honey-Lime Glaze.

Serving: 4-6 | Preparation Time: 10 minutes | Ready Time: 25 minutes

Ingredients:
- 4 - 6 fresh salmon filets
- 2 tablespoons olive oil
- Salt & pepper, to taste
- 1/4 cup honey
- Juice of 1/2 lime

Instructions:
1. Preheat grill to medium-high heat.
2. Brush salmon with olive oil and season with salt & pepper.
3. Grill salmon for 4-5 minutes per side or until cooked through to desired doneness.
4. Meanwhile, in a small saucepan, combine honey and lime juice and cook over low heat until glaze reaches a syrup-like consistency.
5. Brush glaze over salmon filets, reserving some for garnish.
6. Serve salmon with the remaining glaze.

Nutrition Information: Per serving: Calories: 350, Total Fat: 18g, Saturated Fat: 3g, Cholesterol: 75mg, Sodium: 80mg, Carbohydrates: 16g, Fiber: 0g, Sugar: 15g, Protein: 28g.

44. Grilled Portobello Mushrooms with Balsamic Glaze

This delicious Grilled Portobello Mushrooms with Balsamic Glaze is an easy and flavourful dish that will be a hit in any kitchen. Serve it as an appetizer or a side dish to your main course.

Serving: 4 | Preparation Time: 10 minutes | Ready Time: 15 minutes

Ingredients:

- 4 large sized portobello mushrooms
- 2 tablespoons balsamic vinegar
- 2 tablespoons olive oil
- Salt and pepper to taste
- 2 tablespoons minced garlic

Instructions:
1. Preheat the grill to medium-high heat.
2. Remove any dirt or debris from the mushrooms and pat them dry with a paper towel.
3. In a small bowl, combine balsamic vinegar, olive oil, salt and pepper, and minced garlic.
4. Brush the mixture on both sides of the mushrooms.
5. Grill the mushrooms for 4-5 minutes per side until they are tender and lightly charred.
6. Once cooked, drizzle with the remaining balsamic glaze and serve.

Nutrition Information (per serving):
Calories: 104, Fat: 7g, Protein: 3g, Carbohydrates: 8g, Fiber: 2.5g, Sugars: 5g, Sodium: 38mg

45. Grilled Cheese Sandwiches with Tomato Jam

Grilled Cheese Sandwiches with Tomato Jam combine creamy cheese, sweet and tangy tomatoes, with buttery grilled bread to create the ultimate blend of cheesy goodness.

Serving: 4| Preparation Time: 10 minutes| Ready Time: 15 minutes

Ingredients:
- 4 slices of crusty bread
- 2 tablespoons of butter
- 4 slices of cheddar cheese
- 1/4 cup of tomato jam

Instructions:
1. Preheat a large skillet over medium heat.
2. Spread butter onto one side of each slice of bread.

3. Place the bread, butter side down, in the pan.
4. Layer the cheese onto each piece of bread.
5. Spread the tomato jam on top of the cheese.
6. Place the remaining slices of bread, butter side up, onto the sandwiches.
7. Grill for 2-3 minutes, or until bread is golden brown and cheese is melted.
8. Flip sandwiches and grill for another 2-3 minutes, until both sides are golden brown.
9. Serve and enjoy.

Nutrition Information:
Calories: 343, Fat: 17g, Carbohydrates: 34g, Protein: 12g, Sodium: 604mg, Fiber: 2g.

46. Grilled Jerk Chicken Drumsticks

Grilled Jerk Chicken Drumsticks – This delicious Caribbean-inspired Jerk Chicken Drumsticks recipe is full of flavor with an addictive kick. The sticky marinade is bursting with spices, herbs and citrus and grilling it to perfection will give your chicken an irresistible great taste. Serve with a side of coleslaw for a complete meal.

Serving: 4 | Preparation Time: 10 minutes | Ready Time: 40 minutes

Ingredients:
- 8 chicken drumsticks
- 2 tablespoons olive oil
- 2 tablespoons Jerk seasoning

Instructions:
1. Place the drumsticks into a large bowl.
2. In a separate bowl, add the olive oil and jerk seasoning; mix together until well blended.
3. Pour the jerk marinade over the chicken, and rub in the mixture.
4. Chill the chicken in the refrigerator for at least 30 minutes.
5. Preheat your grill on medium-high heat.

6. Add the chicken drumsticks to the hot grill and cook for 20-25 minutes, turning frequently, until chicken is cooked through.

Nutrition Information (per serving):
Calories: 250 Fat: 14g Cholesterol: 90 mg Sodium: 700 mg Carbohydrates: 3 g Fiber: 1 g Protein: 28 g

47. Grilled Cheese and Avocado Quesadillas

This flavorful and easy to make Grilled Cheese and Avocado Quesadillas dish is sure to be a hit! Bursting with sharp cheddar, creamy avocado and flavorful spices, you can have this delicious snack ready in just 25 minutes.

Serving: 4| Preparation Time: 10 minutes| Ready Time: 15 minutes

Ingredients
- 8-inch flour tortillas
- 1/2 cup shredded cheddar cheese
- 1/4 cup chopped green onions
- 1 cup mashed avocado
- 1 teaspoon chopped fresh jalapeno
- 2 tablespoons olive oil
- Salt and pepper, to taste

Instructions
1. Preheat a grill or skillet over medium-high heat.
2. In a bowl, mix together the cheddar cheese, green onions, mashed avocado, and jalapeno.
3. Place a flour tortilla on the hot grill or skillet. Spread the chees and avocado mixture over one side of the tortilla.
4. Fold the tortilla in half, pressing down gently to seal the edges.
5. Grill, flipping every few minutes, until cheese is melted and tortilla is lightly browned and crispy, about 15 minutes.
6. Remove from heat and repeat with remaining tortillas and filling.

Nutrition Information
Per Serving:

Calories: 259 kcal
Fat: 15.3 g
Carbohydrates: 21.3 g
Protein: 10 g
Sodium: 543 mg
Sugar: 1.4 g

48. Grilled Halibut Fillets with Mango Salsa

This fresh and flavorful grilled halibut fillets with mango salsa is the perfect summertime meal. The sweetness of the mango salsa combined with the char of the grilled fish creates an amazing outdoor dining experience.

Serving: 4| Preparation Time: 10 minutes| Ready Time: 20 minutes

Ingredients:
-4 skinless halibut fillets
-1 ripe mango, peeled, pitted and diced
-1 red bell pepper, diced
-Jalapeno pepper, minced
-3 Tablespoons freshly squeezed lime juice
-2 Tablespoons finely chopped fresh cilantro
-1 Tablespoon Olive oil
-1 garlic clove, minced
-Salt and pepper to taste

Instructions:
1. Preheat an outdoor grill to medium-high heat.
2. Wash and pat dry the fillets, and then season with salt and pepper.
3. Grill the fillets for 4 minutes per side.
4. In a small bowl, combine the diced mango, red bell pepper, jalapeno, lime juice, cilantro, olive oil and garlic.
5. Mix well and season to taste with salt and pepper.
6. Top the grilled halibut with the mango salsa.

Nutrition Information:

Calories: 218 | Total Fat: 6.3 g | Saturated Fat: 1.0g | Cholesterol: 94mg | Sodium: 119mg | Total Carbohydrates: 7.6g | Dietary Fiber: 2.6g | Protein: 30.4g

49. Grilled Squash and Zucchini with Mango Sauce

Grilled Squash and Zucchini with Mango Sauce is a delicious summertime dish that brings together the sweet and tangy flavor of mangoes with the savory taste of grilled vegetables. With just a few simple ingredients and a short prep and cook time, this dish is sure to be a hit at your next barbecue or family gathering.

Serving: 6| Preparation Time: 10 minutes| Ready Time: 20 minutes

Ingredients:
- 2 medium zucchini, cut into thin slices
- 2 medium yellow squash, cut into thin slices
- 2 tablespoons olive oil
- 1/2 teaspoon garlic powder
- Salt and pepper, to taste
- 2 tablespoons butter
- 2 ripe mangos, peeled and diced
- 2 tablespoons honey
- 2 tablespoons lime juice
- Chopped cilantro, for garnish (optional)

Instructions:
1. Preheat the grill to medium-high.
2. Toss the zucchini and squash slices with the olive oil, garlic powder, salt and pepper.
3. Place the vegetables on the grill and cook on each side for 4-5 minutes or until nicely charred.
4. Melt the butter in a medium saucepan over medium heat and add the mangoes. Cook for 2-3 minutes, stirring often.
5. Add the honey and lime juice and cook for 1-2 more minutes, stirring often. Remove from the heat.
6. Serve the grilled squash and zucchini with the mango sauce and garnish with chopped cilantro, if desired.

Nutrition Information:
Calories: 145 kcal, Carbohydrates: 13 g, Protein: 1 g, Fat: 9 g, Saturated Fat: 4 g, Cholesterol: 15 mg, Sodium: 101 mg, Potassium: 264 mg, Fiber: 1 g, Sugar: 11 g, Vitamin A: 510 IU, Vitamin C: 24 mg, Calcium: 17 mg, Iron: 2 mg.

50. Grilled Beer-Battered Fish and Chips

This recipe for Grilled Beer-Battered Fish and Chips is sure to make for an exquisite meal. A crunchy, crispy beer-battered fish combined with flavorful oven-baked chips are sure to be hit with the whole family!

Serving: 4-6 people | Preparation Time: 30-35 minutes | Ready Time: 35-40 minutes

Ingredients:
-1 lb cod fillets
-1/2 tsp garlic powder
-1/2 tsp paprika
-1/2 tsp sea salt
-1 cup all-purpose flour
-3/4 cup light beer
-1/2 cup bread crumbs
-1/2 tsp smoked paprika
-1/2 tsp garlic powder
-1/2 tsp dried oregano
-3-4 russet potatoes, cut into wedges
-Sea salt and pepper, to taste
-2 tablespoons olive oil

Instructions:
1. Preheat the oven to 425 degrees F. Line a baking sheet pan with parchment paper.
2. In a shallow bowl, mix together the garlic powder, paprika, and sea salt. Rub the mixture onto both sides of the cod fillets until evenly coated.

3. In a separate shallow bowl, mix together the flour, beer and bread crumbs until there are no lumps and a thick batter is formed.
4. Dip the cod into the batter, and ensure that the fillets are fully coated. Place the battered cod on the prepared baking sheet.
5. In a separate bowl, mix together the smoked paprika, garlic powder, dried oregano, sea salt and pepper. Drizzle the olive oil over the potatoes and toss until evenly coated. Then, sprinkle the spices blend over the potatoes and toss until evenly coated. Arrange the potatoes on the baking sheet alongside the cod, then bake in the oven for 25–30 minutes until golden.
6. Serve the grilled beer-battered fish and chips with your favorite condiments and/or sides. Enjoy!

Nutrition Information:
Calories: 387 kcal; Carbohydrates: 45 g; Protein: 21 g; Fat: 14 g; Saturated Fat: 2 g; Cholesterol: 34 mg; Sodium: 609 mg; Potassium: 669 mg; Fiber: 4 g; Sugar: 1 g; Vitamin A: 138 IU; Vitamin C: 20 mg; Calcium: 48 mg; Iron: 4 mg.

51. Grilled Lamb Kebabs with Mint Pesto

Grilled Lamb Kebabs with Mint Pesto is a flavor-packed meal worthy of a special occasion. Juicy pieces of marinated lamb are skewered with vegetables, then grilled until charred and cooked through. The vibrant mint pesto makes an indulgent dipping sauce that can't be beat!

Serving: 4 | Preparation Time: 30 minutes | Ready Time: 45 minutes

Ingredients:
-10 ounces Ground Lamb
-1 zucchini, cut into cubes
-1 red onion, cut into wedges
-1 large bell pepper, cut into cubes
-1 Tablespoon olive oil
-2 Tablespoons chopped fresh oregano
-2 teaspoons cumin
-2 teaspoons smoked paprika
-Salt and pepper

-1/4 cup Olive Oil
-1/4 cup Fresh Mint leaves
-2 cloves garlic
-2 Tablespoons pine nuts
-2 Tablespoons Parmesan cheese

Instruction:
1. Heat a gas grill to medium-high heat (or heat a grill pan over medium-high heat).
2. In a large bowl, combine the lamb, zucchini, red onion, bell pepper, olive oil, oregano, cumin, smoked paprika, 1 teaspoon salt, and 1/2 teaspoon pepper until everything is evenly distributed.
3. Form the mixture into 8 even kebabs and skewer with 4-inch wooden or metal skewers.
4. Grill the skewers until the lamb is cooked through, 5-7 minutes.
5. Meanwhile, make the pesto: in a food processor, combine the olive oil, mint, garlic, pine nuts, Parmesan, and 1/2 teaspoon salt. Blend until creamy and smooth.
6 .Serve the kebabs with the pesto.

Nutrition Information:
Calories: 300, Total Fat: 23g, Saturated Fat: 6g, Cholesterol: 45mg, Sodium: 400mg, Total Carbohydrates: 6g, Dietary Fiber: 2g, Sugar: 2g, Protein: 15g

52. Grilled Polenta with Parmesan Cheese

This delicious Grilled Polenta with Parmesan Cheese is an easy vegetarian meal that packs a punch of flavour. It is a tasty way to enjoy the deliciously nutty taste of polenta and the pleasingly sharp flavour of Parmesan cheese.

Serving: 4| Preparation Time: 10 minutes| Ready Time: 30 minutes

Ingredients:
- 500g Polenta
- 3 tablespoons Olive Oil
- 2 cloves Garlic, minced

- 2 tablespoons Parmesan Cheese
- A dash of Sea Salt
- 1/2 teaspoon Black Pepper

Instructions:
1. Preheat your oven to 350F.
2. Grease a baking sheet with the olive oil.
3. Spread the polenta on the baking sheet.
4. Sprinkle the garlic, Parmesan cheese, salt and pepper over the polenta and spread it evenly.
5. Bake in the oven for 25-30 minutes or until the top is golden and the polenta is cooked through.
6. Remove from the oven and cool for a few minutes before cutting into squares.
7. Heat a lightly greased grill pan or outdoor grill over medium-high heat.
8. Grill the polenta on both sides until lightly browned and crunchy.
9. Serve warm and enjoy!

Nutrition Information:
Serving Size: 1 of 4 servings
Calories: 131 kcal
Carbohydrates: 19 g
Protein: 3 g
Fat: 6 g
Saturated Fat: 1 g
Cholesterol: 2 mg
Sodium: 244 mg
Potassium: 87 mg
Fiber: 2 g
Sugar: 0 g
Vitamin A: 0.6%
Vitamin C: 0.1%
Calcium: 5.5%
Iron: 5.5%

53. Grilled Quinoa Stuffed Peppers

Grilled Quinoa Stuffed Peppers is a simple and delicious vegan-friendly dish, perfect for sharing with family and friends. Whether you choose to serve it as a main course, or as a side dish, this is a great way to get your fill of protein and fiber while making a flavorful and colorful meal.

Serves: 4, | Preparation Time: 15 minutes, | Ready Time: 25 minutes.

Ingredients:
- 2 large bell peppers, halved lengthwise and seeds removed
- 1/2 cup quinoa, cooked
- 1/2 cup diced veggies of choice (mushrooms, zucchini, tomatoes, etc)
- 2 cloves garlic, minced
- 2 tablespoons fresh herbs of choice, chopped
- 2 tablespoons extra virgin olive oil
- 1 teaspoon smoked paprika
- 1/4 teaspoon each sea salt & freshly ground black pepper

Instructions:
1. Preheat your grill to medium-high heat.
2. Place prepared bell peppers on the grill and cook for 6-8 minutes, or until slightly charred.
3. Meanwhile, in a large bowl, combine cooked quinoa, veggies, garlic, herbs, olive oil, smoked paprika, salt, and pepper.
4. After the peppers have cooked, fill each one with the quinoa mixture, and place back on the grill.
5. Cook for an additional 10 minutes, or until the quinoa is cooked through and the peppers are tender.

Nutrition Information:
Total Calories: 183 | Protein: 4.7g | Carbohydrates: 24.1g | Dietary Fiber: 3.6g | Total Fat: 8.9g | Sodium: 168mg

54. Grilled Potato Skins with Cheddar Cheese

Grilled Potato Skins with Cheddar Cheese is a delicious dish that brings together potatoes, cheese, and herbs to create a flavorful side dish or appetizer. This dish takes roughly 15 minutes to prepare and 35 minutes to cook, serving 4 people.

Serving: 4| Preparation Time: 15 minutes| Ready Time: 35 minutes

Ingredients:
- 4 baking potatoes
- 2 tablespoons butter, melted
- 1/2 teaspoon salt
- 1/4 teaspoon pepper
- 1/2 cup shredded cheddar cheese
- 2 tablespoons chopped fresh chives

Instructions:
1. Preheat the oven to 375 F.
2. Scrub and pat dry the potatoes, then prick each one with a fork.
3. Place the potatoes on a baking sheet. Bake for 40 minutes, or until tender.
4. Remove potatoes from the oven and cool them for 10 minutes.
5. Cut the potatoes in half and scoop out the flesh, leaving about 1/4 inch of potato inside the skins.
6. Brush the potato skins with melted butter and season with salt and pepper.
7. Top each potato skin with shredded cheese and chopped chives.
8. Place the potatoes on a baking sheet and bake for another 15 minutes until golden brown and the cheese is melted.

Nutrition Information:
Calories: 238kcal
Carbohydrates: 20.3g
Protein: 9.3g
Fat: 13.5g
Saturated Fat: 7.8g
Cholesterol: 34mg
Sodium: 412mg
Potassium: 510mg
Fiber: 1.7g
Sugar: 0.6g
Calcium: 152mg
Iron: 0.9mg

55. Grilled Sweet Potato Hash with Chorizo

This flavorful Grilled Sweet Potato Hash with Chorizo is the perfect brunch dish. It's packed with spices and prepared in only twenty minutes. It's packed with flavor, making it a great way to start the day.

Serving Size: 4 | Preparation Time: 10 minutes | Ready Time: 20 minutes

Ingredients:
- 2 sweet potatoes, peeled and cut into 1/2-inch cubes
- 1 red bell pepper, diced
- 1/2 white onion, diced
- 1/2 teaspoon smoked paprika
- 1/2 teaspoon ground cumin
- 2 tablespoons olive oil
- OT teaspoon coarse salt
- 1/4 teaspoon freshly ground black pepper
- 4 ounces fresh chorizo
- 1/4 cup sliced scallions

Instructions:
1. Heat a charcoal or gas grill to medium-high heat.
2. In a large bowl, combine the diced sweet potatoes, bell pepper, onion, smoked paprika, cumin, olive oil, salt and pepper. Toss to combine.
3. Grill the sweet potato mixture, stirring occasionally, for about 6 minutes.
4. Add the chorizo to the grill, and cook for an additional 2-3 minutes, stirring occasionally.
5. Serve the Grilled Sweet Potato Hash with Chorizo topped with sliced scallions.

Nutrition Information (per serving)
Calories: 206
Fat: 14g
Cholesterol: 24mg
Sodium: 408mg
Carbohydrates: 14.6g
Protein: 6g

56. Grilled Apple and Brie Quesadillas

Grilled Apple and Brie Quesadillas are a unique and delicious combination of sweet and savory. A simple and tasty way to use up leftover crusty bread, this quesadilla is grilled to perfection and can be served as a snack, appetizer, or light meal.

Serving: Makes 2 Quesadillas | Prep Time: 10 minutes | Ready Time: 15 minutes

Ingredients:
- 2 large tortillas
- 3 tablespoons butter, melted
- 1/4 cup diced apple
- 1/4 cup brie cheese

Instructions:
1. Preheat a skillet to medium heat.
2. Brush one side of the tortilla with melted butter.
3. Place the buttered side down onto the skillet.
4. Sprinkle the diced apple and brie cheese onto the tortilla.
5. Cover with the other tortilla, brush the top with melted butter.
6. Grill for 2-3 minutes until the bottom side is golden brown.
7. Flip the quesadilla and grill for another 2-3 minutes, or until the other side is golden brown.
8. Cut the quesadilla into wedges and serve.

Nutrition Information:
Calories: 337, Fat: 19g, Saturated Fat: 12g, Cholesterol: 44mg, Sodium: 1604mg, Carbohydrates: 35g, Fiber: 2g, Protein: 6g

57. Grilled Asparagus and Mushroom Kebabs

This flavorful and simple Grilled Asparagus and Mushroom Kebab recipe is perfect for any outdoor BBQ event. They can be served as a side, appetizer, or even a main dish. They're incredibly versatile and full of protein and fiber.

Serves 4. | Preparation Time: 10 minutes. | Ready Time: 25 minutes.

Ingredients:
- 1 bunch of asparagus
- 8 cremini mushrooms
- 2 tablespoons olive oil
- 1 teaspoon garlic powder
- 1/2 teaspoon ground black pepper
- 1/2 teaspoon sea salt

Instructions:
1. Preheat the grill to medium-high heat.
2. Trim and discard the woody ends from the asparagus, then cut into 1-inch pieces.
3. Clean and trim the cremini mushrooms and slice into halves or quarters.
4. Place the vegetables in a large bowl and add the olive oil, garlic powder, black pepper, and sea salt. Toss and evenly coat the vegetables.
5. Thread the vegetables onto kebab skewers and place them on the preheated grill.
6. Grill for 8-10 minutes, turning the kebabs occasionally, until they are tender and lightly charred.

Nutrition Information:
- Calories – 126 kcal
- Protein – 5 g
- Carbs – 9 g
- Fat – 8 g
- Fiber – 5 g
- Sugar – 2 g

58. Grilled Eggplant Burgers with Pesto

Grilled Eggplant Burgers with Pesto is an easy and delicious meal made with healthy ingredients and flavorful pesto! This vegan-friendly dish makes four servings and is ready in 45 minutes.

Serving: 4| Preparation Time: 30 minutes | Ready Time: 45 minutes

Ingredients:
- 2 eggplants
- 4 burger buns
- 2 tablespoons olive oil
- 1/3 cup vegan pesto
- 2 teaspoons garlic powder
- Salt and pepper
- 2/3 cup shredded vegan mozzarella

Instructions:
1. Preheat an outdoor grill to medium heat.
2. Slice the eggplants into 1/2 inch rounds, then brush with olive oil on each side.
3. Place eggplant slices on the hot grill and sprinkle with garlic powder and salt and pepper. Grill for 5 minutes on each side.
4. Once cooked, spread pesto and vegan mozzarella on each cooked eggplant burger, then place on top of the buns and cover with top bun.
5. Serve and enjoy!

Nutrition Information:
Calories: 175
Fat: 10.4g
Carbohydrates: 22.7g
Protein: 3.8g

59. Grilled Pineapple with Chili-Lime Glaze

Grilled Pineapple with Chili-Lime Glaze is an easy and tasty summertime treat that offers both sweet and spicy flavors. The glaze, made with chili powder, lime juice, brown sugar and butter, adds a unique twist to fresh pineapple slices that have been grilled over medium high heat. This recipe serves four, and is ready in just 25 minutes.

Serving: 4 | Preparation Time: 10 minutes | Ready Time: 25 minutes

Ingredients:
- 2 ripe pineapples, peeled, cored and cut into 1-inch thick slices

- 2 tablespoons butter
- 1 teaspoon chili powder
- 1/4 cup fresh lime juice
- 2 tablespoons light brown sugar

Instructions:
1. Preheat a grill to medium-high heat.
2. Grill the pineapple slices for 3-4 minutes each side or until lightly charred.
3. In a small saucepan, melt the butter over low heat.
4. Add the chili powder and lime juice and stir together until combined.
5. Add the brown sugar and continue to stir until the sugar has dissolved.
6. Remove the glaze from the heat and brush it over the grilled pineapple slices.
7. Serve the grilled pineapple slices with the chili-lime glaze over the top.

Nutrition Information: Per Serving (1/4 of Recipe): 222 calories, 8g fat, 1g saturated fat, 34g carbohydrate, 2g protein, 4g dietary fiber, 11mg cholesterol, 28mg sodium

60. Grilled Orange-Ginger Pork Chops

Grilled Orange-Ginger Pork Chops are a tasty and easy-to-make dish that's perfect for a summertime barbecue! This dish combines flavorful pork chops marinated in orange juice and ginger, then grilled on the barbeque until crispy on the outside and juicy on the inside.

Serving: 4| Preparation Time: 10 minutes| Ready Time: 25 minutes

Ingredients:
- 4 boneless pork chops
- 1 cup orange juice
- 2 tablespoons minced ginger
- 1 teaspoon garlic powder
- Salt and pepper, to taste
- 2 tablespoons olive oil

Instructions:

1. In a medium bowl, whisk together orange juice, ginger, garlic powder, salt, and pepper.
2. Place pork chops in a shallow dish, then pour the marinade over. Cover and allow to marinate for at least 15 minutes (up to 4 hours).
3. Heat a grill over medium-high heat.
4. Brush pork chops with olive oil. Place on the grill and cook for about 4 minutes per side, flipping the chops halfway through.
5. When cooked through, remove the pork chops from the grill and serve.

Nutrition Information (per serving):
Calories: 378, Protein: 25g, Carbohydrates: 5g, Sugar: 4g, Fat: 24g, Fiber: 0g, Sodium: 256mg

61. Grilled Curried Vegetables with Peanuts

This delicious and nutritious grilled curried vegetables with peanuts dish is a perfect side for any meal and a great way to get your recommended daily intake of vegetables. Serving this dish with rice or flat bread makes it an interesting, flavorsome and complete meal.

Serving: 4-6 | Preparation Time: 15 minutes | Ready Time: 20 minutes

Ingredients:
- 1 red pepper, cut into chunks
- 2 carrots, cut into sticks
- 1 onion, cut into chunks
- 1 courgette, cut into chunks
- 1 red onion, cut into wedges
- 2 tablespoons of curry powder
- 1/2 teaspoon of ground cumin
- 3 tablespoons of honey
- 2 tablespoons of sesame oil
- 3 tablespoons of peanut butter
- 3 tablespoons of tamari soy sauce
- 3 tablespoons of toasted peanuts

Instructions:
1. Preheat a grill to medium heat, or turn on an outdoor grill.
2. In a large bowl, mix together the peppers, carrots, onions, courgette, and red onions.
3. In a smaller bowl, mix together the curry powder, cumin, honey, sesame oil, peanut butter, tamari soy sauce, and peanuts until a paste is formed.
4. Generously coat the vegetables with the paste and mix until evenly distributed.
5. Place the vegetables onto a tray and place onto the grill for about 10-15 minutes, turning occasionally, until the vegetables are cooked through.
6. Serve immediately with extra peanuts and a sprinkle of sesame oil.

Nutrition Information:
Calories: 312, Fat: 14.7g, Protein: 8.5g, Carbs: 35.4g, Dietary Fiber: 5.1g

62. Grilled Vegetable Ratatouille with Goat Cheese

Grilled Vegetable Ratatouille with Goat Cheese is a delicious vegetarian dish that is sure to please any crowd. It's a beautiful layering of grilled vegetables on a bed of goat cheese, finished off with a light balsamic glaze. This dish is healthy and easy to make, with just 15 minutes of | Preparation Time. Serve it as a side or an entrée and it's sure to become an instant favorite.

Serving: 4-6 | Preparation Time: 15 minutes | Ready Time: 30 minutes

Ingredients:
- 2 tablespoons olive oil
- 1 small red onion, finely chopped
- 2 small carrots, finely chopped
- 2 cloves garlic, minced
- 2 zucchinis, cut into small cubes
- 1 red bell pepper, cored and in thin slices
- 2 yellow squash, cut into small cubes
- 1 stalk of celery, finely chopped
- 1 eggplant, cut into small cubes
- 1 teaspoon dried oregano

- 1 teaspoon dried basil
- 2 tablespoons balsamic vinegar
- 2 tablespoons of goat cheese, crumbled
- Salt and pepper to taste

Instructions:
1. Preheat the oven to 375 degrees Fahrenheit.
2. Heat olive oil in a large pot over medium heat. Add the onions, carrots, garlic and celery and cook for about 5 minutes, stirring frequently.
3. Add the zucchini, bell pepper, eggplant, oregano, and basil and cook for an additional 5 minutes.
4. Add the balsamic vinegar and season with salt and pepper.
5. Transfer the mixture to a baking dish and spread the goat cheese on top.
6. Bake for 15 minutes, or until the vegetables are tender.

Nutrition Information (per serving):
Calories: 120
Fat: 10g
Carbs: 8g
Protein: 4g
Fiber: 4g

63. Grilled Coconut-Lime Chicken Breasts

This flavorful Grilled Coconut-Lime Chicken Breasts recipe is perfect for a summer BBQ or cookout. The combination of sweet and savory elements creates a unique and delicious dish that everyone will love.

Serving: 8 | Preparation Time: 5 minutes | Ready Time: 30 minutes

Ingredients:
-2-3 chicken breasts
-1 cup coconut milk
-2 limes, juiced
-1 teaspoon ground ginger
-1 teaspoon ground cumin

-1 teaspoon smoked paprika
-Sea salt, to taste
-Freshly cracked black pepper, to taste

Instructions:
1. In a medium bowl, whisk together the coconut milk, lime juice, ginger, cumin, and paprika until blended.
2. Place chicken in a large shallow baking dish or sealable plastic bag. Pour the marinade over the chicken, cover and refrigerate at least 1 hour.
3. Heat an outdoor or stovetop grill to medium-high heat.
4. Remove the chicken from refrigerator and season each side with salt and pepper.
5. Grill the chicken 4 minutes per side, or until a meat thermometer placed in the center of the breast reads 165F.
6. Remove from the grill and serve warm.

Nutrition Information:
Serving size: 1 chicken breast
Calories: 198
Fat: 10 g
Saturated fat: 8 g
Carbohydrates: 6 g
Sugar: 5 g
Fiber: 1 g
Protein: 21 g
Cholesterol: 53 mg
Sodium: 58 mg

64. Grilled Coconut-Lime Shrimp Skewers

Grilled Coconut-Lime Shrimp Skewers are a quick and flavorful dish perfect for entertaining or weeknight meals. This summery recipe takes just 15 minutes to prepare and creates a delicious, zesty shrimp dish the whole family will love.

Serving: 4| Preparation Time: 15 minutes| Ready Time: 15 minutes

Ingredients:

- 2 1/2 tablespoons olive oil
- 1 tablespoon freshly squeezed lime juice
- 1 1/2 teaspoons lime zest
- 1/2 teaspoon garlic powder
- 1/4 teaspoon cayenne pepper
- 1/4 teaspoon sea salt
- 2 cloves garlic, minced
- 1 pound large shrimp, shelled and deveined
- 30 ounces unsweetened coconut flakes

Instructions:
1. Preheat the grill to medium heat.
2. In a medium bowl, whisk together the olive oil, lime juice, lime zest, garlic powder, cayenne pepper, sea salt, and garlic.
3. Add the shrimp to the bowl and toss to coat.
4. In a separate shallow bowl, spread the coconut flakes.
5. Working one at a time, thread the shrimp onto metal or wooden skewers.
6. Roll the skewered shrimp in the coconut flakes and thoroughly press it into the shrimp.
7. Grill the skewers for 3-4 minutes per side, or until the shrimp is cooked through.

Nutrition Information: Serving size: 1/4 of recipe, Calories: 339, Fat: 17.3g, Saturated Fat: 14.3g, Cholesterol: 183mg, Sodium: 257mg Carbohydrates: 17.3g, Fiber: 4.5g, Sugar: 5.6g, Protein: 27.5g

65. Grilled Chicken Tostadas with Pickled Onions

Grilled Chicken Tostadas with Pickled Onions are a delicious and easy way to have a filling meal in no time. The mix of thick, crunchy tostada shells with savory marinated chicken, creamy mayo, and sweet pickled onions is absolutely mouthwatering.

Serves: 4 | Preparation Time: 15 minutes | Ready in: 30 minutes

Ingredients:
- 4 tostada shells

- 18 oz chicken breast, marinated and grilled
- 1/4 cup mayonnaise
- 2 tablespoons pickled onions
- Sea salt and freshly ground black pepper
- 1 teaspoon olive oil

Instructions:
1. Preheat oven to 375F.
2. Place tostada shells on a baking sheet.
3. Heat a cast iron or nonstick pan over medium heat and add the olive oil.
4. Add the chicken to the pan and cook until golden brown and cooked through.
5. Place the tostada shells in the oven and bake for 7 minutes or until golden and crispy.
6. Remove from oven and top each tostada with grilled chicken, a tablespoon of mayo, and a tablespoon of pickled onions.
7. Season with salt and pepper to taste.

Nutrition Information:
- Calories: 433
- Fat: 21g
- Saturated Fat: 4g
- Cholesterol: 88mg
- Sodium: 545mg
- Carbohydrates: 28g
- Fiber: 6g
- Sugar: 4g
- Protein: 36g

66. Grilled Coconut-Ginger Salmon Steaks

This Grilled Coconut-Ginger Salmon Steaks dish brings together mellow coconut, spicy ginger and the sweetness of honey to create an unforgettable flavor combination. This easy-to-make meal is perfect for a summer evening.

Serve for 4. | Preparation Time: 10 minutes. | Ready Time: 30 minutes.

Ingredients:
- 4 salmon steaks
- 2 tablespoons coconut cream
- 1 teaspoon grated fresh ginger
- 2 tablespoons honey
- Salt and black pepper
- 2 tablespoons vegetable oil

Instructions:
1. Preheat a barbecue to medium heat, or preheat the oven to 375 degrees F (190 degrees C).
2. In a shallow bowl, combine the coconut cream, ginger, honey, salt and pepper.
3. Place the salmon steaks into the coconut and ginger mixture, making sure that all sides are evenly coated.
4. Heat the oil in a large skillet over medium-high heat.
5. Place the salmon steaks in the hot oil and cook for about 5 minutes on each side until golden brown.
6. Move the salmon steaks onto a lightly oiled baking sheet or dish and bake for about 20 minutes or until the fish flakes easily with a fork.

Nutrition Information:
- Calories: 294 kcal
- Carbohydrates: 11.4 g
- Protein: 30 g
- Fat: 14.4 g
- Saturated Fat: 7.5 g
- Cholesterol: 85 mg
- Sodium: 172 mg
- Potassium: 886 mg
- Fiber: 0.9 g
- Sugar: 10.1 g

67. Grilled Cornbread with Maple-Jalapeno Butter

Take savory-sweet cornbread to a new level with this flavorful Grilled Cornbread with Maple-Jalapeno Butter recipe. The butter is savory and slightly sweet, with a hint of spice. A fantastic side dish that requires minimal prep, this is the perfect accompaniment to any meal.

Serving: 8 | Preparation Time: 10 minutes | Ready Time: 25 minutes

Ingredients:
1 cup cornmeal
1 teaspoon baking powder
1 teaspoon baking soda
1/2 teaspoon salt
1 cup buttermilk
1 egg
1/4 cup butter
1/4 cup maple syrup
2 tablespoons minced jalapeno pepper

Instructions:
1. Preheat a gas or charcoal grill to medium-high heat.
2. In a medium mixing bowl, whisk together the cornmeal, baking powder, baking soda, and salt.
3. In a separate bowl, whisk together the buttermilk, egg, and butter.
4. Pour the wet ingredients over the dry ingredients and mix until just combined.
5. Ladle the batter into a greased 8-inch round cake pan.
6. Place the pan on the hot grill and cook for 15 minutes or until the edges turn golden brown.
7. Meanwhile, in a small bowl, mix together the maple syrup and jalapeno pepper.
8. Once the cornbread is cooked, spread the maple-jalapeno butter over top and cut into 8 slices.

Nutrition Information: Calories: 181, Total Fat: 8 g, Saturated Fat: 5 g, Cholesterol: 41 mg, Sodium: 353 mg, Total Carbohydrate: 24 g, Dietary Fiber: 1 g, Protein: 3 g

68. Grilled Nectarine and Blue Cheese Salad

This light and flavorful Grilled Nectarine and Blue Cheese Salad is a summer favorite. It is simple to make and is packed full of nutrition.

Serving: 3 | Preparation Time: 10 mins | Ready Time: 15 mins

Ingredients:
-3 ripe nectarines
-3 tablespoons olive oil, plus extra for drizzling
-1/4 cup crumbled blue cheese
-2 tablespoons freshly chopped basil leaves
-2 tablespoons white balsamic vinegar
-1/4 teaspoon salt
-1/4 teaspoon freshly ground black pepper

Instructions:
1. Preheat a grill pan or outdoor grill to medium heat.
2. Slice nectarines in half and brush with olive oil. Grill for 4 minutes each side.
3. Place grilled nectarines on a plate and sprinkle with blue cheese, basil, salt and pepper.
4. Drizzle with olive oil and white balsamic vinegar.

Nutrition Information:
Calories - 171, Fat – 12g, Saturated Fat – 2.5g, Cholesterol – 4mg, Sodium – 325mg, Carbs – 13.4g, Sugar – 10.8g, Fiber – 2g, Protein – 3.3g

69. Grilled Feta and Tomato Kebabs

Grilled Feta and Tomato Kebabs are a delicious and healthy summer dish, combining protein-packed feta with fresh tomato chunks. Topped with a sprinkle of fresh herbs, they make a quick, easy and incredibly delicious lunch or dinner.

Serving: 4 | Preparation Time: 10 minutes | Ready Time: 20 minutes

Ingredients:
- 1/2 lb feta cheese, cut into 12 cubes

- 2 large tomatoes, cut into 12 chunks
- 4 tbsp olive oil
- 2 tsp dried oregano
- 1 tsp salt
- 1/2 tsp freshly ground pepper

Instructions:
1. Preheat your grill to high heat.
2. In a bowl, combine the feta cubes, tomato chunks, olive oil, oregano, salt and pepper. Toss to coat evenly.
3. On each of four skewers, load three feta cubes and three tomato chunks, alternating, to make four kebabs.
4. Place the kebabs on the preheated grill and cook for 10 minutes, or until the feta is golden brown and the tomatoes are slightly charred.
5. Serve warm, and garnish with additional herbs if desired.

Nutrition Information – per serving (4 servings):
Calories: 238
Fat: 18g
Protein: 9g
Carbs: 6g
Fiber: 1g
Sodium: 902mg

70. Grilled Eggplant and Roasted Red Pepper Sandwich

This delicious and vegetarian friendly Grilled Eggplant and Roasted Red Pepper Sandwich is easy to make and will be a great addition to your lunch or dinner menu.

Serving:This recipe serves 2.| Preparation Time:15 minutes| Ready Time:45 minutes

Ingredients:
- 2 eggplants
- 2 roasted red peppers, sliced

- 2 garlic cloves, minced
- 2 tablespoons olive oil
- 1 teaspoon sea salt + black pepper
- 2 tablespoons balsamic vinegar
- 2 tablespoons fresh lemon juice
- 4 slices of bread

Instructions:
1. Preheat your oven to 400F (200°C).
2. Slice the eggplants into 1/2-inch rounds and lay them on a parchment paper-lined baking sheet. Drizzle the eggplant slices with olive oil and season with sea salt and black pepper.
3. Roast the eggplant slices in the preheated oven for 25 minutes.
4. In a small bowl, mix together the balsamic vinegar, lemon juice, garlic, and a pinch of salt and pepper.
5. While the eggplants are roasting, prepare the roasted red peppers by slicing them into thin strips.
6. Once the eggplants are roasted, assemble the sandwiches with the roasted red peppers, eggplant, and your favorite bread.
7. Drizzle the balsamic vinegar and lemon juice mixture over the sandwiches and enjoy.

Nutrition Information:
This sandwich provides approximately 200 calories per serving, and is a good source of dietary fiber, vitamin C, and potassium.

71. Grilled Flank Steak with Caramelized Onions

This delicious and easy to make classic steak dish pairs juicy grilled flank steak with sweet and savory caramelized onions. Serve it with your favorite sides for a delectable weeknight dinner.

Serving: 4| Preparation Time: 10 minutes| Ready Time: 25 minutes

Ingredients:
- 2 lbs flank steak
- 2 tbsp olive oil
- 2 onions, thinly sliced

- 2 tbsp butter
- 2 tsp sugar
- 1 tsp Worcestershire sauce
- Salt and pepper to taste

Instructions:
1. Heat a large skillet or griddle over medium heat. Rub the steak with olive oil and season both sides with salt and pepper to taste.
2. Cook the flank steak for 4 minutes on each side for medium rare.
3. Transfer to a plate and cover to keep warm.
4. Add the butter and onions to the skillet and season with salt and pepper. Cook, stirring occasionally, until the onions become golden brown and caramelized, about 10 minutes.
5. Add the sugar and Worcestershire sauce and stir until combined.
6. Serve the steak with the caramelized onion topping.

Nutrition Information:
Calories: 409; Total fat: 25.3g; Saturated fat: 10.2g; Cholesterol: 95mg; Sodium: 84mg; Carbohydrates: 12g; Protein: 32g; Fiber: 1.2g.

72. Grilled Balsamic-Glazed Portobello Mushroom

Grilled Balsamic-Glazed Portobello Mushrooms is a savory and delicious dish that can be prepared in no time. It is a perfect meal to grill in the summertime, with balsamic glaze imparting a burst of flavor.

Serves 4, | Preparation Time 10 minutes, | Ready time 20 minutes.

Ingredients:
- 4 portobello mushroom caps
- 2 tablespoon balsamic vinegar
- 1 teaspoon olive oil
- 2 cloves garlic, minced
- 1 teaspoon Italian seasoning
- Salt and pepper to taste

Instructions:
1. Preheat grill for medium-high heat.

2. Combine balsamic vinegar, olive oil, garlic, Italian seasoning, salt and pepper in a small bowl to make marinade.
3. Brush each portobello mushroom cap with the marinade.
4. Grill mushrooms for 12-15 minutes until cooked through and browned.
5. Serve hot, with additional balsamic glaze if desired.

Nutrition Information:
- Calories: 107
- Total Fat: 5g
- Saturated Fat: 1g
- Sodium: 142mg
- Potassium: 325mg
- Total Carbohydrates: 11g
- Dietary Fiber: 2g
- Sugars: 5g
- Protein: 5g

73. Grilled Whole Trout with Lemon-Ginger Butter

Grilled Whole Trout with Lemon-Ginger Butter is a quick, easy and healthy way to enjoy fish. Perfect for a summer barbecue, it offers a delicious combination of sweet and savory flavors.

Serving: 4 | Preparation Time: 10 minutes | Ready Time: 20 minutes

Ingredients:
- 4 whole trout
- 2 tablespoons butter
- 2 tablespoons fresh lemon juice
- 1 tablespoon grated ginger
- 1 teaspoon garlic powder
- Salt and pepper to taste
- 2 tablespoons fresh chopped cilantro (optional)

Instructions:
1. Preheat the grill to medium-high heat.

2. Place the butter in a small bowl and soften. Add the lemon juice, grated ginger and garlic powder to the bowl and mix together.
3. Season the trout with salt and pepper on both sides.
4. Place the trout on the preheated grill and cook for 10 minutes, flipping halfway through.
5. Once the trout is cooked through, brush with the lemon-ginger butter mixture.
6. Garnish with cilantro if desired.

Nutrition Information (per serving):
Calories: 200; Total Fat: 10 g; Saturated Fat: 5 g; Cholesterol: 90 mg; Sodium: 190 mg; Carbohydrates: 1 g; Protein: 29 g.

74. Grilled Bacon-Wrapped Beef Tenderloin

Grilled Bacon-Wrapped Beef Tenderloin is a delicious and flavorful dish that will be sure to impress your dinner guests. The beef tenderloin is wrapped in bacon, grilled to juicy perfection and bursting with flavor.

Serves 8. | Preparation Time 25 minutes. | Ready in 1 hour.

Ingredients:
- 2-pound beef tenderloin
- 16 slices bacon
- 1 tablespoon garlic powder
- 1 teaspoon mustard
- 2 tablespoons Worcestershire sauce
- Salt and black pepper, to taste

Instructions:
1. Preheat the grill to medium-high heat.
2. Wrap the beef tenderloin in bacon strips and secure with toothpicks.
3. Combine the garlic powder, mustard, Worcestershire sauce, salt and black pepper in a small bowl.
4. Brush the bacon-wrapped beef with the mixture.
5. Place the beef on the preheated grill and cook for approximately 20 minutes, or until the internal temperature reaches 145F.
6. Let the beef tenderloin rest before slicing.

Nutrition Information:
Serving size 1/8 of beef tenderloin. Calories 308, Total Fat 22g, Cholesterol 81mg, Sodium 624mg, Total Carbohydrate 1g, Protein 21g.

75. Grilled Mozzarella Sticks with Pesto

Enjoy the classic combination of gooey melted mozzarella and pesto in grilled mozzarella cheese sticks. The grilled cheese sticks are coated in pesto, making this a delicious snack or appetizer.

Serving: 8 | Preparation Time: 15 minutes | Ready Time: 10 minutes

Ingredients:
-2 cups of diced mozzarella cheese
-2 tablespoons of pesto
-1 egg
-1/4 cup of breadcrumbs
-1 teaspoon of garlic powder
-1 tablespoon of olive oil

Instructions:
1. Preheat your grill or a grill pan to medium-high heat.
2. In a small bowl combine breadcrumbs, garlic powder, and salt and pepper.
3. In a separate bowl beat the egg.
4. Dip individual mozzarella cubes into egg, then coat with breadcrumb mix.
5. Place cheese cubes on the grill and cook for 2-3 minutes per side until cheese is melted.
6. Once cheese is melted, remove from grill and drizzle with pesto.
7. Serve and enjoy!

Nutrition Information: Serving size 1 mozzarella cheese stick. Calories 90, Total fat 5.5g, Sat. fat 2.4g, Cholesterol 25mg, Sodium 160mg, Total Carbohydrate 5g, Dietary fiber 0g, Sugars 0g, Protein 6g.

76. Grilled Potato Salad with Bacon and Sage

Grilled Potato Salad with Bacon and Sage is a hearty side dish that combines the flavorful crunch of bacon, the intense flavor of fresh sage, and the comforting texture of warm grilled potatoes. With just a few simple ingredients and a few minutes of cooking time, you can whip up a delicious potato salad that your entire family will love.

Serving: 8 | Preparation Time: 10 Minutes | Ready Time: 25 Minutes

Ingredients:
- 6 slices of bacon
- 2 pounds potatoes
- 2 tablespoons olive oil
- 2 tablespoons chopped sage
- 2 tablespoons red wine vinegar
- 2 tablespoons Dijon mustard
- 2 tablespoons minced shallots
- Salt and pepper to taste

Instructions:
1. Preheat your grill to medium-high heat.
2. Cut the potatoes into 1-inch pieces and toss with the olive oil and salt and pepper.
3. Place the potatoes in a single layer on the grill and cook until tender and lightly charred, 5-7 minutes per side.
4. Meanwhile, cook the bacon in a large skillet until crisp. Remove the bacon to a paper-towel lined plate.
5. Once the potatoes are done, transfer them to a large bowl and add the bacon, sage, red wine vinegar, Dijon mustard, and shallots and toss until combined.

Nutrition Information:
- Calories: 205
- Fat: 8.8g
- Carbs: 19.4g
- Protein: 6.9g

77. Grilled Chicken, Mushroom and Spinach Wraps

Grilled Chicken, Mushroom and Spinach Wraps are a wholesome and delicious dish, loaded with flavor. They make great lunch or dinner wraps and are very easy to make.

Serving: 8 wraps | Preparation Time: 15 minutes | Ready Time: 30 minutes

Ingredients:
- 2 grilled chicken breasts, thinly sliced
- 2 tablespoons olive oil
- 2 cloves garlic, minced
- 2 cups mushrooms, sliced
- 2 cups spinach, chopped
- 8 large tortilla wraps
- Salt and pepper to taste

Instructions:
1. Heat olive oil in a large skillet over medium heat.
2. Add garlic and mushrooms and cook for 3-4 minutes, stirring often.
3. Add spinach and cook for 2 minutes more.
4. Add the cooked chicken and stir together.
5. Season with salt and pepper, to taste.
6. Divide chicken mixture equally between the 8 tortilla wraps.
7. Roll up each wrap and grill on a panini grill or in a large skillet for about 5 minutes.

Nutrition Information: Per serving (1 wrap): Calories - 248, Fat - 8.6g, Protein - 16.3g, Carbohydrates - 25.6g, Cholesterol - 28.3mg, Sodium - 462mg.

78. Grilled Peach Crumble with Cinnamon-Walnut Streusel

Savory, sweet, and with an unexpected punch of spiced crunch: Grilled Peach Crumble with Cinnamon-Walnut Streusel is the perfect summertime dessert.

Serving: 8-10 | Preparation Time: 15 minutes | Ready Time: 1 hour

Ingredients:
- 6-8 ripe peaches, halved, pitted and skin removed
- 2 tablespoons coconut oil
- 1/2 cup coconut sugar
- 2 tablespoons of lemon juice
- 1 teaspoon ground cinnamon
- 1/2 teaspoon almond extract
- 1 teaspoon of sea salt

Streusel Topping:
- 1/2 cup walnuts, chopped
- 1/4 cup tapioca or arrowroot flour
- 1/4 cup coconut sugar
- 2 tablespoons ground cinnamon
- 2 tablespoons melted coconut oil

Instructions:
1. Heat grill to medium-high. Lightly brush the cut side of each peach half with coconut oil.
2. Place the peaches, cut-side down, on the grill and cook for about 4-8 minutes per side. Remove once you see nice grill marks and the peaches are softened.
3. Transfer the grilled peaches to a 9x13-inch baking dish. Sprinkle the coconut sugar, lemon juice, cinnamon, almond extract, and sea salt over the peaches.
4. In a medium bowl, mix together the walnuts, tapioca or arrowroot flour, coconut sugar, and cinnamon. Stir to combine. Then add the melted coconut oil and stir again until the mixture forms small crumbly pieces.
5. Sprinkle the streusel topping over the peaches in the baking dish.
6. Bake at 350 degrees for 45 minutes or until the crumble is golden brown, and the edges are bubbly.
7. Serve warm with a dollop of coconut or regular Greek yogurt.

Nutrition Information:
Calories – 220 kcal, Carbohydrates – 27g, Fat – 13.2g, Protein – 2.7g, Sodium – 173mg

79. Grilled Gorgonzola and Sausage-Stuffed Mushrooms

Grilled Gorgonzola and Sausage-Stuffed Mushrooms make for a rich, creamy and flavorful bite-size appetizer. This recipe is both simple and delicious, making it the perfect addition to any gathering or backyard cookout.

Serving: 10 | Preparation Time: 20 minutes | Ready Time: 25 minutes

Ingredients:
- 10 large white mushrooms
- 1/2 cup ground sausage
- 1/4 cup Gorgonzola cheese
- 1/4 cup freshly chopped parsley
- 2 tablespoons olive oil
- Salt and pepper to taste

Instructions:
1. Preheat your grill to medium-high heat.
2. Carefully remove the mushroom stems. Make sure to leave the mushroom cap intact.
3. In a medium-size bowl, mix together the sausage, Gorgonzola cheese, parsley, olive oil, salt and pepper.
4. Fill each mushroom cap with the sausage and cheese mixture.
5. Place the stuffed mushrooms on the preheated grill and cover.
6. Grill the mushrooms for approximately 10 minutes, or until the mushrooms are tender and the cheese is melted.
7. Remove from the grill and serve.

Nutrition Information (per serving):
Calories: 145
Fat: 10 g
Carbs: 1 g
Protein: 11 g

80. Grilled Fish Tacos with Mango Salsa

Introducing Grilled Fish Tacos with Mango Salsa – the perfect combination of delicious grilled fish and fruity sweetness! A quick and easy meal perfect for any night of the week.

Serving: 4 tacos | Preparation Time: 5 minutes | Ready Time: 15 minutes

Ingredients:
- 2 tablespoons olive oil
- 2 firm white fish fillets
- 1 teaspoon chili powder
- 4 small tortillas
- 2 cups fresh hard mango, diced
- 1/4 cup red onion, finely diced
- 1/4 cup cilantro, chopped
- 2 tablespoons jalapeno, diced
- Juice from 1 lime
- Salt to taste

Instructions:
1. Heat one tablespoon of olive oil in a pan over a medium-high heat.
2. Season fish with chili powder, salt, and pepper and place in the heated pan.
3. Cook for 4-5 minutes on each side until it's lightly browned and cooked through.
4. Remove fish from pan and dice into small cubes.
5. In a bowl, add mango, red onion, cilantro, jalapeno, lime juice, and a pinch of salt and mix well.
6. To assemble the tacos, place two tablespoons of diced fish onto each tortilla, then top with the mango salsa.
7. Drizzle the remaining tablespoon of olive oil over the tacos and enjoy!

Nutrition Information:
Calories: 199; Total Fat: 8 g; Cholesterol: 36 mg; Sodium: 196 mg; Total Carbohydrates: 15 g; Protein: 14 g; Fiber: 2 g; Sugars: 6 g.

81. Grilled Romaine and Avocado Salad

Grilled Romaine and Avocado Salad is a delicious and light dish perfect for any lunch or dinner. The creamy avocado and salty parmesan cheese compliment the grilled Romaine perfectly.

Serving: 4 | Preparation Time: 10 minutes | Ready Time: 20 minutes

Ingredients:
- 2 heads of Romaine lettuce, cut into quarters
- 2 avocados, diced
- 4 tablespoons olive oil
- 2 tablespoons freshly squeezed lime juice
- 2 tablespoons freshly grated Parmesan cheese
- 1/4 teaspoon garlic powder
- Salt and pepper to taste

Instruction:
1. Preheat an outdoor grill to medium-high heat.
2. Brush romaine lettuce quarters with olive oil.
3. Place romaine lettuces on the preheated grill, and cook for 4 minutes per side.
4. Place grilled romaine into a bowl, and mix with diced avocados.
5. In a separate bowl, whisk together the lime juice, Parmesan cheese, garlic powder, salt, and pepper.
6. Drizzle the dressing over the grilled romaine and avocado mix, and stir to combine.

Nutrition Information:
Per serving: Calories 265, Total Fat 25g, Saturated Fat 4g, Cholesterol 5mg, Sodium 145mg, Carbohydrates 9g, Fiber 5g, Sugars 0g, Protein 6g

82. Grilled Watermelon Salad with Feta

A hearty and uplifting salad dish, this Grilled Watermelon Salad with Feta combines protein-rich feta with sweet, juicy watermelon slices that have been grilled to bring out their flavor. A colorful side dish or light meal, this fresh and flavorful grilled watermelon salad is sure to please.

Serving: 4 | Preparation Time: 5 minutes | Ready Time: 20 minutes

Ingredients:
- 5 cups cubed watermelon
- 2 tablespoons olive oil
- 2 tablespoons lemon juice
- 5 oz feta cheese, crumbled
- 2 tablespoons chopped parsley
- 2 tablespoons chopped mint
- 1 red onion, thinly sliced
- salt and pepper, to taste

Instruction:
1. Preheat a grill or grill pan to medium-high heat.
2. In a large bowl, combine cubed watermelon, olive oil and lemon juice and toss to coat.
3. Place the watermelon chunks on the grill and cook for 4-6 minutes, until lightly charred.
4. Place the grilled watermelon in a large bowl. Add the remaining ingredients and mix to combine.
5. Serve and enjoy!

Nutrition Information:
Calories: 161; Fat: 8g; Carbs: 18g; Protein: 5g; Sodium: 326mg; Sugar: 12g

83. Grilled Asparagus and Prosciutto Skewers

These Grilled Asparagus and Prosciutto Skewers are full of flavor and texture. The asparagus is grilled until crisp yet tender and the salty prosciutto adds delightful contrast.

Serving: 4-5 skewers | Preparation Time: 10 minutes | Ready Time: 20 minutes

Ingredients:
- 12 asparagus spears

- 2-4 oz prosciutto
- 2 tablespoons olive oil
- 2 cloves garlic, minced

Instructions:
1. Preheat the grill or grill pan over medium-high heat.
2. Wash and dry the asparagus spears and cut them in half.
3. Cut the prosciutto in half lengthwise, then cut each piece into thirds.
4. Mix the garlic and olive oil together in a small bowl.
5. Thread two pieces of prosciutto, the cut side of the asparagus, and additional prosciutto on a skewer.
6. Brush the skewers with the olive oil mixture.
7. Grill the skewers for 3-5 minutes on each side.
8. Serve and enjoy.

Nutrition Information: Serving size: 1 skewer; Calories: 76; Carbohydrates: 1.5g; Protein: 5.2g; Fat: 5.8g; Sodium: 159mg; Sugar: 0.5g.

84. Grilled Chicken Caesar Salad Wraps

Grilled Chicken Caesar Salad Wraps are an incredibly delicious and easy meal to make. Packed with ample fresh vegetables and a lemony, garlic dressed salad, this meal is sure to please all taste buds.

Serving: Makes 4 wraps | Preparation Time: 10 minutes | Ready Time: 20 minutes

Ingredients:
-4 chicken breasts
-1 head Romaine lettuce, washed and chopped
-4 wraps
-4 tablespoons olive oil
-4 tablespoons freshly squeezed lemon juice
-2 cloves garlic, minced
-2 tablespoons grated parmesan cheese
-Salt and pepper to taste

Instructions:

1. Preheat the grill to medium heat.
2. Brush chicken breasts with olive oil. Season with salt and pepper to taste.
3. Grill the chicken for 8-10 minutes, turning occasionally until fully cooked.
4. In a small bowl, combine olive oil, lemon juice, garlic and parmesan. Season with salt and pepper.
5. On each wrap, layer Romaine lettuce evenly, top with chicken and drizzle dressing over top.
6. Fold up wrap and enjoy!

Nutrition Information: Per wrap – Calories 263, Fat 11.1g, Carbs 21.6g, Protein 18.4g.

85. Grilled Cheese and Apple Kebabs

Grilled Cheese and Apple Kebabs are an easy and delicious way to combine sweet and savory flavors in one delicious snack. With just a few ingredients and only a few minutes' | Preparation Time, you'll be ready to enjoy this scrumptious combination in no time.

Serving: 6 | Preparation Time: 10 minutes | Ready Time: 10 minutes

Ingredients
- 6 wooden skewers
- 6 slices of cheese
- 2 apples, cored and diced
- 2 tablespoons of butter, melted

Instructions
1. Preheat a grill or pan to medium-high heat.
2. Skewer one piece of cheese and one piece of diced apple onto each skewer in an alternating pattern, until all the skewers are filled.
3. Brush the melted butter onto both sides of each kebab.
4. Place the skewers onto the preheated grill or pan and cook for 3 to 4 minutes, or until the cheese is nicely melted.
5. Turn the skewers and cook for another 3 minutes, or until the cheese is fully melted and the apples are softened and lightly browned.

Nutrition Information
- Calories: 120
- Fat: 8 grams
- Carbs: 5 grams
- Protein: 6 grams

86. Grilled Artichoke and Tomato Bruschetta

Grilled Artichoke and Tomato Bruschetta is a tasty appetizer that is perfect for game day, family gatherings, or any kind of party. This delicious dish combines chopped artichokes with freshly grilled tomatoes and mixed herbs, served on top of crispy toasted bread.

Serving: 6-8 | Preparation Time: 10 minutes | Ready in: 25 minutes

Ingredients:
- 2 large tomatoes, sliced
- 2 teaspoons olive oil
- 1 tablespoons balsamic vinegar
- 6 canned artichoke hearts, drained and chopped
- 2 garlic cloves, minced
- 2 tablespoons freshly minced parsley
- 2 tablespoons freshly minced basil
- 2 tablespoons freshly minced oregano
- Salt and pepper to taste
- 4 slices of French bread or similar, toasted

Instructions:
1. Preheat the grill to medium-high heat.
2. In a medium bowl, mix together the tomato slices, olive oil, balsamic vinegar, artichoke hearts, garlic, parsley, basil, oregano, salt and pepper.
3. Place the tomato and artichoke mixture onto the grill and cook for 5-7 minutes, stirring occasionally.
4. Toast the French bread slices for several minutes until golden brown.
5. Top the toasted bread slices with the grilled artichoke and tomato mixture.
6. Serve and enjoy!

Nutrition Information (per serving):
Calories: 173 kcal
Carbohydrates: 19g
Protein: 7g
Fat: 8g
Sodium: 183mg
Fiber: 4g

87. Grilled Tilapia with Mango-Lime Salsa

This flavorful Grilled Tilapia with Mango-Lime Salsa is an easy and delicious dish that is perfect for any occasion. The salsa adds a zesty and fruity kick while the grilled fish leaves it light and easy to eat.

Serving: 4 | Preparation Time: 15 minutes | Ready Time: 35 minutes

Ingredients:
- 4 tilapia fillets
- 1 teaspoon olive oil
- 1/4 teaspoon salt
- 1/4 teaspoon ground pepper
- 1/2 mango, diced
- 2 tablespoons fresh lime juice
- 2 tablespoons chopped fresh cilantro
- 1 tablespoon red onion, minced

Instructions:
1. Preheat the grill to medium-high heat.
2. Rub the tilapia fillets with olive oil, salt, and pepper.
3. Grill for 4-5 minutes per side.
4. In a small bowl, mix together mango, lime juice, cilantro, and red onion until combined.
5. Serve the grilled tilapia with the mango-lime salsa.

Nutrition Information (per serving):
Calories: 119
Total Fat: 3g

Carbohydrates: 5g
Protein: 17g

88. Grilled Vegetable Skewers with Balsamic Glaze

This easy and delicious vegetable side dish is full of flavor, featuring a savory balsamic glaze. Perfect for summer barbecues and easy enough to make any time of year.

Serving: 4-6 | Preparation Time: 10 minutes | Ready Time: 25 minutes

Ingredients:
- 1/2 red pepper, cut into 1-inch pieces
- 1/2 yellow pepper, cut into 1-inch pieces
- 1/2 orange pepper, cut into 1-inch pieces
- 1 small red onion, cut into 1-inch pieces
- 1 zucchini, cut into 1-inch pieces
- 1 yellow squash, cut into 1-inch pieces
- 1/4 cup olive oil
- 1/4 cup balsamic vinegar
- 2 cloves garlic, minced
- 2 tablespoons chopped fresh basil
- Salt and pepper, to taste

Instructions:
1. Preheat your grill to medium-high heat.
2. Thread the vegetables onto metal or wooden skewers, alternating them.
3. In a medium bowl, whisk together the olive oil, balsamic vinegar, garlic, basil, salt, and pepper until emulsified.
4. Brush the skewers with the balsamic glaze.
5. Grill the skewers on the preheated grill until the vegetables are slightly charred and cooked through, about 10 minutes, turning occasionally and brushing with the glaze while they grill.

Nutrition Information: Per Serving (1 skewer with balsamic glaze) - 48 calories, 3.2 g fat, 3.3 g carbohydrates, 0.8 g protein, 0.5 g fiber.

89. Grilled Pineapple Bread Pudding with Rum-Caramel Sauce

Grilled Pineapple Bread Pudding with Rum-Caramel Sauce is a warm, comforting dessert perfect for those cool nights. It's an ooey-gooey treat topped with a delicious rum-caramel sauce. It's sure to be a hit with family and friends!

Serving: 6-8 | Preparation Time: 20 minutes | Ready Time: 40 minutes

Ingredients:
- 4 cups cubed stale bread
- 1/2 cup butter, melted
- 2 cups fresh pineapple, chopped
- 1/4 cup dark brown sugar
- 2 eggs
- 2 cups half-and-half
- 2 tablespoons dark rum
- 1 tablespoon pure vanilla extract
- 1 teaspoon ground cinnamon
- 1/4 cup granulated sugar

Instructions:
1. Preheat the grill to 375F.
2. Place the bread cubes in a large bowl and pour the melted butter over them, stirring to coat.
3. In a separate bowl, mix together the chopped pineapple, brown sugar, eggs, half-and-half, rum, vanilla extract, and cinnamon.
4. Add the bread cubes and stir to combine.
5. Grease a 9x13-inch baking dish and pour the bread pudding mixture into it. Sprinkle the top with the granulated sugar.
6. Place the baking pan on the preheated grill and close the lid. Grill for 30 minutes, or until the bread pudding is set and golden brown on top.
7. Allow the bread pudding to cool slightly before serving topped with your favorite caramel sauce or rum-caramel sauce.

Nutrition Information: This Grilled Pineapple Bread Pudding with Rum-Caramel Sauce per serving contains approxmately 201 calories, 10.7

grams of fat, 3.3 grams of saturated fat, 22.4 grams of carbohydrates, and 2.9 grams of protein.

90. Grilled Prosciutto-Wrapped Scallops

Grilled Prosciutto-Wrapped Scallops – An easy yet gourmet appetizer or main course that will impress your guests. A wonderful combination of salty prosciutto with sweet, succulent scallops, these scallops are sure to be a hit.

Serving: 8 | Preparation Time: 10 minutes | Ready Time: 15 minutes

Ingredients:
- 8 large sea scallops
- 4 slices of prosciutto, halved
- 2 tablespoons olive oil
- Salt, to taste
- Fresh ground black pepper

Instructions:
1. Preheat the grill over medium-high heat.
2. Carefully wrap each scallop with half a slice of prosciutto.
3. Drizzle the scallops with olive oil and season with salt and pepper.
4. Place the prosciutto-wrapped scallops on the preheated grill, and cook for 5 minutes per side, until the prosciutto is crispy and the scallops are cooked all the way through.

Nutrition Information (per serving):
Calories: 138 | Fat: 7.9g | Protein: 10.7g | Carbohydrates: 0.7g | Fiber: 0g | Sugar: 0g

91. Grilled Corn on the Cob with Chili-Lime Butter

This Grilled Corn on the Cob with Chili-Lime Butter is a flavorful spin on the classic summer side dish. Enjoyed best on a summer evening, this dish is sure to tantalize your taste buds and liven up your summer!

Serving: 6 | Preparation Time: 10 minutes | Ready Time: 10 minutes

Ingredients:
-6 ears of corn
-3 tablespoons of butter, melted
-1 lime
-1 teaspoon of chili powder
-2 tablespoons of chopped fresh cilantro (optional)
-Salt and pepper

Instructions:
1. Preheat the grill to medium high heat.
2. Peel back the husks on the corn, removing the silks, and then re-wrap the husks around the corn.
3. Place the corn on the grill and cook with the lid closed, turning the corn occasionally, for 8-10 minutes, or until the husks turn golden.
4. Remove the corn from the grill and allow to cool slightly.
5. Meanwhile, In a small bowl mix together the melted butter, lime juice, chili powder, cilantro, salt, and pepper.
6. Peel back the husks from the corn and brush the chili-lime butter over the top.
7. Serve warm either with additional chili-lime butter or just as is.

Nutrition Information:
Calories: 120; Fat: 6g; Sodium: 50mg; Carbohydrates: 17g; Protein: 3g; Fiber: 3g.

92. Grilled Potato Wedges with Garlic-Herb Butter

This savory side dish of Grilled Potato Wedges with Garlic-Herb Butter is bursting with flavor and perfect as an accompaniment to any meal - whether it be savory steak, juicy chicken, or flavorful seafood.

Serving: 4-6 | Preparation Time: 15 minutes | Ready Time: 25 minutes

Ingredients:
- 2.5 pounds of small potatoes, cut into wedges
- 4 tablespoons of olive oil

- 2 garlic cloves, minced
- 2 tablespoons of butter, melted
- 2 tablespoons of fresh chopped herbs of choice, like thyme, rosemary, oregano, etc.
- Ground black pepper
- Kosher salt

Instructions:
1. Preheat grill to medium-high heat.
2. Place potato wedges in a large bowl. Add olive oil and garlic and toss until wedges are evenly coated.
3. Place wedges on the hot grill, close the lid and allow to cook for 10-15 minutes, flipping the wedges halfway through cooking until they are cooked through and lightly charred.
4. Remove the wedges from grill and place on a large plate.
5. In a small bowl, mix together butter, herbs, pepper and salt until evenly incorporated.
6. Drizzle the wedges with the herb-butter and enjoy!

Nutrition Information (per serving):
120 calories; 10g fat; 3g saturated fat; 8g carbohydrate; 1.3g dietary fibre; 1.3g sugar; 1.5g protein

93. Grilled Kebabs with Apricot-Chipotle Glaze

Grilled Kebabs with Apricot-Chipotle Glaze are full of flavor and require minimal time to prepare. These juicy and irresistible kebabs are perfect for any summer BBQ.

Serving: 8 | Preparation Time: 20 minutes | Ready Time: 45 minutes

Ingredients:
- 2 pounds boneless, skinless chicken breasts, cut into 1 1/2-inch cubes
- 1/2 cup apricot preserves
- 1/4 cup finely chopped chipotle peppers in adobo sauce
- 2 tablespoons lime juice
- 2 tablespoons olive oil
- 2 tablespoons minced fresh cilantro

- 1 teaspoon chili powder
- 2 cloves garlic, minced
- 1/4 teaspoon salt
- Wooden skewers, soaked in water for 30 minutes

Instructions:
1. Preheat grill to medium-high heat.
2. In a large bowl, whisk together the apricot preserves, chipotle peppers, lime juice, olive oil, cilantro, chili powder, garlic, and salt.
3. Place the chicken cubes in the marinade and stir to coat. Let the chicken sit in the marinade mixture for at least 20 minutes.
4. While the chicken is marinating, thread the cubes onto wooden skewers.
5. Grill the chicken skewers for 8-10 minutes, or until the chicken is cooked through and the outside is lightly charred.
6. Serve immediately.

Nutrition Information:
Calories: 235; Total Fat: 6 grams; Saturated Fat: 1 gram; Cholesterol: 95 milligrams; Sodium: 350 milligrams; Carbs: 13 grams; Fiber: 1 gram; Protein: 30 grams.

94. Grilled Cheese Sandwich with Caramelized Onions

Grilled cheese sandwiches with caramelized onions make for an incredibly delicious and satisfying meal. With a combination of complex and sweet flavors, this delightful sandwich is great for lunch, dinner, or a snack.

Serving: Makes 4 sandwiches | Preparation Time: 10 minutes | Ready Time: 15 minutes

Ingredients:
- 4 slices of your favorite sandwich bread
- 8 ounces of cheese, such as cheddar, Swiss, or Gruyere
- 4-6 tablespoons of butter at room temperature
- 2 large onions, thinly sliced

- Salt
- Pepper
- 2 tablespoons of olive oil

Instructions:
1. Heat the olive oil in a large skillet over medium heat.
2. When the oil is hot, add the onions and season with salt and pepper.
3. Cook the onions until they are golden brown and caramelized, stirring occasionally, about 15 minutes.
4. Meanwhile, butter one side of each slice of bread. Place two slices of bread, buttered side down, on a cutting board.
5. Top each piece of bread with 1/4 of the cheese and then top with 1/4 of the caramelized onions.
6. Place the other two slices of bread on top, buttered side up.
7. Heat a large skillet over medium heat. When the skillet is hot, add the sandwiches.
8. Cook the sandwiches for 3-4 minutes on each side, or until the cheese is melted and the bread is golden brown and crispy.
9. Slice the sandwiches in half and enjoy.

Nutritional Information (per serving): Calories: 396, Fat: 24 g, Carbohydrates: 26 g, Protein: 16 g, Fiber: 2 g, Sodium: 549 mg

95. Grilled Tuna with Wasabi-Lime Mayonnaise

Grilled Tuna with Wasabi-Lime Mayonnaise is a flavorful and light meal that is perfect for any occasion. The subtle flavor of grilled tuna combined with the zesty and spicy kick from the Wasabi-Lime Mayonnaise creates a perfectly balanced flavor profile.

Serving: 2 servings | Preparation Time: 10 minutes | Ready Time: 20 minutes

Ingredients:
- 2 (8 oz) fresh tuna steaks
- 2 tablespoons olive oil
- 2 tablespoons fresh lime juice
- 2 teaspoons wasabi paste

- 2 tablespoons mayonnaise
- Salt and freshly ground pepper

Instructions:
1. Preheat an outdoor or indoor grill over medium-high heat.
2. Brush both sides of the tuna steaks with olive oil, and season with salt and pepper. Grill for about 3 minutes on each side, or until cooked through and no longer pink inside.
3. In a small bowl, whisk together lime juice, wasabi paste, and mayonnaise.
4. Serve tuna steaks with Wasabi-Lime Mayonnaise and enjoy.

Nutrition Information:
Calories: 468; Total Fat: 24g; Saturated Fat: 4g; Cholesterol: 88mg; Sodium: 336mg; Total Carbohydrate: 4g; Dietary Fiber: 0g; Protein: 59g

96. Grilled Spinach and Feta Salad

This Grilled Spinach and Feta Salad is a bright and flavorful salad for your next cookout. The grilled vegetables and feta cheese bring crunch and savory flavor and the homemade lemon-basil dressing ties the dish together.

Serving: 4| Preparation Time: 10 minutes| Ready Time: 20 minutes

Ingredients:
- 2 cups baby spinach
- 1 cup feta cheese
- 1 large bell pepper, cut into strips
- 1 large red onion, cut into wedges
- 2 tablespoons olive oil
- 1 tablespoon lemon juice
- 1 clove garlic, minced
- 1 teaspoon fresh basil, minced
- Salt and pepper to taste

Instructions:
1. Heat grill to medium-high heat.

2. Brush bell pepper and onion with olive oil and season with salt and pepper. Place on grill and cook for about 6 minutes per side, until brown and slightly charred. Remove from heat and set aside.
3. In a small bowl, whisk together lemon juice, garlic, basil, salt, and pepper.
4. In a large bowl, combine spinach, feta cheese, bell pepper, and onion. Pour dressing over the salad and toss to combine.
5. Serve immediately.

Nutrition Information:
Calories: 142, Total Fat: 9g, Saturated Fat: 4g, Cholesterol: 21mg, Sodium: 250mg,Carbohydrates: 10g, Fiber: 2g, Protein: 5g

97. Grilled Fennel with Mascarpone Cheese

Grilled Fennel with Mascarpone Cheese is a delicious and flavorful dish made with fennel, mascarpone cheese, and other seasonings for added flavor. This dish is ideal for any time of the year and pairs perfectly with a variety of side dishes. Serve this dish as a side or appetizer and enjoy!

Serving: 4| Preparation Time: 15 minutes| Ready Time: 25 minutes

Ingredients:
- 2 bulbs of fennel, sliced
- 2 tablespoons of olive oil
- 3/4 cup of mascarpone cheese
- 2 tablespoons of chopped fresh parsley
- 1 teaspoon of fresh thyme
- 1 teaspoon of fresh rosemary
- Salt and pepper to taste

Instructions:
1. Preheat the grill to medium-high heat.
2. Place the fennel slices onto a plate or baking sheet and drizzle with the olive oil. Season with salt and pepper.
3. Place the fennel slices onto the grill and cook for 8-10 minutes, flipping once throughout, until golden and slightly charred.
4. Remove the fennel from the heat and place onto a platter.

5. Top with the mascarpone cheese, parsley, thyme and rosemary. Season with salt and pepper.
6. Serve hot.

Nutrition Information:
Calories: 142
Carbs: 9.8g
Fat: 10.3g
Protein: 2.8g

98. Grilled Pork Tenderloin with Orange-Honey Glaze

Juicy, tender, and incredibly flavorful, this Grilled Pork Tenderloin with Orange-Honey Glaze is a delicious dish that's sure to impress.

Serving: 4-6 | Preparation Time: 10 minutes | Ready Time: 40 minutes

Ingredients:
-2 (1lb) pork tenderloins
-2 tablespoons olive oil
-1/4 cup honey
-1/4 cup orange juice
-1 teaspoon orange zest
-1 teaspoon garlic powder
-1 teaspoon salt
-1/4 teaspoon black pepper

Instructions:
1. Rub pork tenderloins with 1 tablespoon of olive oil and season with garlic powder, salt and pepper.
2. Heat a grill over medium-high heat and lightly oil the grates. Place the pork tenderloins on the prepared grill and cook for about 10 minutes, flipping once, until lightly charred and cooked through.
3. Meanwhile, in a small bowl combine honey, orange juice, orange zest and remaining 1 tablespoon of olive oil. Whisk until combined.
4. Brush the orange-honey glaze over the pork tenderloins and cook for an additional 5-7 minutes or until glaze is slightly charred and sticky.

5. Let the pork tenderloin rest for 5 minutes before slicing and serving.

Nutrition Information: (per serving)
-Calories: 185
- Fat: 5.3g
-Carbohydrates: 13.9g
-Protein: 21.3g

99. Grilled Banana Split with Chocolate Sauce

This Grilled Banana Split with Chocolate Sauce recipe is an indulgent treat that combines the deliciousness of grilled bananas, creamy ice cream and a decadent chocolate sauce. Deliciously rich and creamy, this dessert is sure to be a hit!

Serving: 4-6 | Preparation Time: 10 minutes | Ready Time: 10 minutes

Ingredients:
- 4-6 Bananas
- 4-6 Scoops of Ice Cream
- 1/2 cup Heavy Cream
- 2 tablespoons Unsalted Butter
- 2 tablespoons Brown Sugar
- 6-8 ounces Semi-sweet Chocolate Chips
- 1 teaspoon Vanilla Extract
- Pinch of Salt

Instructions:
1. Preheat the grill to medium-high heat.
2. Peel and slice the bananas in half lengthwise and brush with butter. Place the bananas on the grill, cook for 2 minutes and flip.
3. Meanwhile, in a small saucepan over low heat, combine the cream, butter, sugar, and chocolate chips. Stir until the mixture is completely smooth and the chocolate chips have melted. Take off the heat and stir in the vanilla and salt.
4. Place the bananas on individual plates or a large platter. Top each one with a scoop of ice cream. Drizzle with the warm chocolate sauce and serve.

Nutrition Information (per serving): Calories: 520, Total Fat: 29g, Saturated Fat: 17g, Cholesterol: 70mg, Sodium: 140mg, Carbohydrates: 62g, Fiber: 5g, Sugars: 36g, Protein: 7g.

CONCLUSION

Cooking outdoors is an enjoyable experience that can be savored all year round. With 99 Blazing Fire Pit Recipes: Delicious Meals for Outdoor Cooking, you now have the tools you need to make outdoor cooking a success, even during unpredictable weather. From all types of meat and seafood, to vegetables and starches, there are recipes for every occasion, regardless of the season.

This cookbook provides helpful advice for getting the most of your outdoor cooking experience, such as fire building, controlling the heat, and the different tools needed for grilling, smoking, and roasting. Even if you are new to outdoor cooking and have never cooked over a fire before, the clear instructions will put your worries at ease.

Sure, this cookbook is full of delicious recipes, but it's much more than that. This collection of recipes glorifies the amazing experience of cooking with fire while celebrating the simple pleasures and flavors of camping, tailgating, and any other occasion that brings family and friends together. Gather around the glow of the fire and enjoy fragrant spices, herbs, and aromas that simmer together over flames, for a truly extraordinary culinary journey that will delight your senses.

With the perfect combination of warmth, comfort, and fun, 99 Blazing Fire Pit Recipes: Delicious Meals for Outdoor Cooking is the perfect guide for the serious griller or the inspired beginner. Discover gourmet tastes while savoring the fresh atmosphere, and transport yourself to a whole new level of outdoor culinary excellence, anytime!

www.ingramcontent.com/pod-product-compliance
Ingram Content Group UK Ltd.
Pitfield, Milton Keynes, MK11 3LW, UK
UKHW051525090525
5847UKWH00023B/505